The Linguistic Atlas of the Upper Midwest, Volume 2

THE LINGUISTIC ATLAS

OF THE

UPPER MIDWEST

In Three Volumes

by

HAROLD B. ALLEN

Volume 2 • University of Minnesota Press 1975

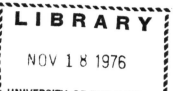
Library of Congress Catalog Card Number: 72-96716
ISBN 0-8166-0756-7

CONTENTS

Chapter 1. Introduction... 3
    The Basis of the Study... 3
    The Social Emphasis of Volume 2................................... 4
    Background Data.. 4
    Presentation of Evidence.. 5
    Supplementary Bibliography.. 5
    Location of Informants (map)...................................... 6
    Phonetic Symbols.. 7
    Abbreviations... 7
    Response Labels... 7
    Appreciation.. 7

Chapter 2. Verbs.. 8
    Tense Forms... 8
    Present Indicative Personal Forms................................32
    Number and Concord...34
    Negative Forms...37
    Infinitive and Present Participle................................43
    Phrases..45

Chapter 3. Nouns...47
    Plurals..47
    Plurals after Numerals...50

Chapter 4. Pronouns..53
    Plurals..53
    Genitives..54
    Relatives..55
    Post-Copula Form...56

Chapter 5. Adjectivals...58

Chapter 6. Articles..60

Chapter 7. Conjunctions..61

Chapter 8. Prepositions..63

Chapter 9. Adverbs...70

Chapter 10. Syntactic Miscellany......................................76

Chapter 11. Addenda...79
    Verbs..79
    Nouns..80
    Pronouns...80
    Adverbials...81
    Adjective and Adverb Comparison..................................81
    Preposition..81
    Multiple Negation..81
    Syntactic Miscellany...81

Chapter 12. Synopsis..83
    Regional Variation...83
    Social Variation...85

Index...89

The Linguistic Atlas of the Upper Midwest, Volume 2

CHAPTER 1

Introduction

The Linguistic Atlas of the Upper Midwest is a study of regional and social variations in the English spoken by native speakers of the language in Minnesota, Iowa, North and South Dakota, and Nebraska. Although it was originally planned in a two-volume format, the *Atlas* now consists of three volumes: 1, The Upper Midwest Project and The Lexicon; 2, The Grammar; 3, The Pronunciation. As a whole, the Upper Midwest project is an independent unit in the series of regional dialect surveys envisaged by Hans Kurath more than three decades ago upon the collapse of the original conception of a unified international investigation that, if it had been realized, would have become the Linguistic Atlas of the United States and Canada.

The findings presented in the three volumes on the Upper Midwest are based upon extensive field interviews with 208 carefully selected local residents representing three generations and three socio-educational groups. Type I informants (infs.) are the oldest. They have had no more than eighth-grade schooling. Type II informants are usually in their fifties or sixties at the time of the interview, with a high school education or its equivalent. Type III informants are younger, with a college or university education gained within the Upper Midwest.

THE BASIS OF THE STUDY

The inclusion of the Type II and Type III informants in the pioneer dialect survey known as the Linguistic Atlas of New England was an important American contribution to dialect research. Earlier European field studies, notably those resulting in the *Atlas linguistique de la France*, had been restricted to the speech of older and relatively uneducated people, chiefly rural. But America, with a less rigid class structure and more rapid social change, presents a quite different situation to the language investigator. To meet this situation Hans Kurath, director of the New England project, included within the surveyed population carefully chosen representative informants offering contrasts both in education and age. Because subsequent American atlas surveys have followed Kurath's lead, American research in dialect geography makes available information about both social and geographical variation.

Of the more than 800 items in the worksheets used by a fieldworker (fw.) during an interview nearly 100 are directed to the matters of grammar and syntax dealt with in this volume. Fieldworkers rarely seek grammatical information by direct questions such as "Do you ever say, 'They was'?" Few persons are reliable reporters of their own grammatical usage. Such information, on the contrary, is usually obtained indirectly, as through questions so phrased as to lead the informant to infer that a lexical item is wanted, or through unfinished questions or statements requiring completion likely to produce the desired grammatical item, or, best of all, in carefully observed free conversation such as for one-half the informants has been preserved on tape recordings.

The vocabulary findings interpreted in Volume 1 relate almost entirely to geographical distribution. As is there made clear, they demonstrate the extension into the Upper Midwest of the major dialect boundaries between the Northern speech characteristics of settlers with backgrounds in western New England, New York State, and northern Ohio, and the Midland speech characteristics of settlers with backgrounds in the Middle Atlantic states, West Virginia, and central Ohio.

The maps in Volume 1 reveal how these two major dialect groups are distributed: Northern speech in Minnesota, North Dakota and northeastern South Dakota, and the northern third of Iowa, and Midland speech in the southern two-thirds of Iowa, southwestern South Dakota, and Nebraska. They also reveal a small invasion of southeastern Iowa by South Midland forms brought there by settlers with family origins in southern Illinois, Kentucky, Tennessee, Virginia, or North Carolina.

Only a few of the vocabulary items in Volume 1 exhibit more than regional contrast. Some terms are identifiable as old-fashioned, even archaic, and hence limited largely to the use of Type I speakers. Only a bare handful manifest clear social-class contrast, as do station and depot, some of the informal equivalents of courting, the use of quiet in expressions meaning "to keep calm," and the compound wiping towel.

THE SOCIAL EMPHASIS OF VOLUME 2

The grammatical matters presented and interpreted in Volume 2 offer a picture sharply different from that in Volume 1. Here the wisdom of Hans Kurath in adding the social dimension to the selection of field informants in American linguistic geography is amply demonstrated.

The variation in grammatical forms in the Upper Midwest does have some correlation with geographical patterns, as evidenced chiefly in the decreased frequency or even absence of certain nonstandard variations in the western half of the area. But more conspicuous is the correlation with the social dimension. The variation exposed and made explicit by the contrasting responses of Type I, Type II, and Type III informants provides major and significant insights into the complex social structuring of American English. Some of these insights appear in the synoptic concluding chapter of this volume.

Data about the strong and other irregular verbs constitute a principal area of social contrast. Nearly all of them occur with variants that, often considered in the schools as either "standard" or "nonstandard" according to a traditional two-valued orientation, actually reveal a much more complicated picture of social contrast along a range from the usage of the educated to that of the uneducated. With some of the variants this range is itself further complicated by regional differences in their distribution.

In order to make comparison easier, the treatment of verbs in this volume is intended to parallel that prepared by the late E. Bagby Atwood and published in 1963 as *A Survey of Verb Forms in the Eastern United States* (VF). Each verb entry in the following pages is listed with the Upper Midwest Atlas worksheet number as identified in Volume 1, and also with cross-reference both to the relevant pages in Atwood's monograph and to the corresponding map in *The Linguistic Atlas of New England* (NE).

BACKGROUND DATA

As in Volume 1, the interpretive description of the distribution of the variants of each verb usually draws upon the background provided by the information in *The Linguistic Atlas of New England*. In addition, it draws upon data from the files of the survey in the Middle and South Atlantic states as described by Atwood and from the files of the linguistic Atlas of the North Central States as summarized in the University of Minnesota doctoral dissertations of Virginia Glenn McDavid ("Verb Forms of the North Central States and Upper Midwest," 1956) and of Jean Malmstrom ("Study of the Validity of Textbook Statements about Certain Grammatical Statements in the Light of Evidence from the Linguistic Atlases," 1958).

Besides the variation in verb forms, a number of other grammatical matters are treated in this volume, such as pronominal forms, noun plurals, and a few syntactic constructions. For them no ready comparison with distribution elsewhere can be drawn except with that in New England and also in Wisconsin, duplicate field records from which state are in the Upper Midwest Atlas office. Data from the Middle and South Atlantic regions exist in field records now being edited at the University of South Carolina for publication by the University of Chicago Press. Data from the other states in the North Central Atlas region await editing at the University of Chicago for publication by the University of Michigan Press. The unfeasibility of consulting these as yet unedited materials makes them practically unavailable until their ultimate publication. However, Professor Raven I. McDavid, Jr., editor of the former collection and co-editor of the latter, has supplied in personal communications certain requested information about a few items, e.g., the plural of moth and the plural of trough.

Certain grammatical variants not sought in the Upper Midwest survey but noted incidentally by fieldworkers during interviews have been included in the Addenda. Some are relevant to the listed categories; some are not. They are recorded here, however, because they do pertain to the facts of social variation in grammatical features.

PRESENTATION OF EVIDENCE

It early was found financially impossible to print in this *Atlas* all the phonetically transcribed replies of all informants to all the items in the worksheets. But the interpretation of the items treated in this volume does cite the specific data that are relied upon as supporting evidence. The evidence appears in one or more of three ways. First, informants who use a given variant are individually identified by their assigned serial numbers: 1-65 for Minnesota, 101-150 for Iowa, 201-226 for North Dakota, 301-328 for South Dakota, and 401-437 for Nebraska. Second, a statistical summary of replies is often given in terms of proportions by informant types and by states. Percentages, of course, are not to be understood as precise indicators. The difference between, say, 62% and 73% is not likely to be very significant. Both are often best interpreted as "about two-thirds." Yet there are occasions when a consistent decrease or increase of a few percentage points between the southern section and the northern section is reasonably interpreted as revelatory of either Midland or Northern orientation. Third, when any regional distribution pattern appears, a map shows the patterning of the responses of those informants using specific variants. Reference to the base map (page 6) will enable the user to determine the exact location of each informant. Further analysis of responses may be easily accomplished by charting them on a map obtained by replicating this base map by any available copying process. For this purpose no permission of the copyright holder is required.

In such a wide-meshed survey as this in the Upper Midwest the results obtained are to be understood as representative of a large area within which individuals or even certain small communities may provide exceptions to the general conclusions. It must be noted, however, that support for the validity of the sample population that was surveyed is to be found in the supplementary mail survey that yielded the replies of 1064 respondents to 136 lexical items as reported in Volume 1. Except for three or four items that are either puzzling or call for special interpretation, the tabulated checklist returns strongly confirm the lexical distribution patterns revealed by the field records. It may reasonably be inferred that equal validity inheres in the grammatical data summarized in this volume.

Volume 1 should also be consulted for further information about the following: history of the project, the population and settlement history of the Upper Midwest, the methods and procedures of dialect research, the worksheet items, the description of the communities and the informants, and the regional dialect patterns made clear by the collected data.

SUPPLEMENTARY BIBLIOGRAPHY

Omitted accidentally from the list of publications utilized in the preparation of Chapter 2 of Volume 1 are the following:

Blegen, Theodore. *Minnesota: A History of the State*. Minneapolis: University of Minnesota Press, 1963.

Christianson, Theodore. *Minnesota, the Land of Sky-Tinted Waters: A History of the State and Its People*. 5 vols. Chicago and New York: American Historical Society, 1935.

Federal Writers' Project. *Iowa: A Guide to the Hawkeye State*. New York: Viking Press, 1938.

Federal Writers' Project. *Minnesota: A State Guide*. New York: Hastings House, 1938.

Federal Writers' Project. *Nebraska: A Guide to the Cornhuskers State*. New York: Viking Press, 1939.

Federal Writers' Project. *North Dakota: A Guide to the Northern Prairie State*. New York: Oxford University Press, 1950.

Jennewin, J. Leonard, and Jane Boorman, eds. *Dakota Panorama*. N.p.: Dakota Territory Centennial Commission, 1961.

Schell, Herbert S. *History of South Dakota*. Lincoln: University of Nebraska Press, 1961.

Sirjamaki, John. "The people of the Mesabi Range." *Minnesota History* 27 (1946), 203-15.

Stubenhaus, Kieve. "The Origins and Growth of the Nebraska Population." M.A. thesis, University of Nebraska, 1935.

Particular attention is directed to the state guides listed above. Although some of their statistics are now outdated, as invaluable sources of background information they have not yet been superseded.

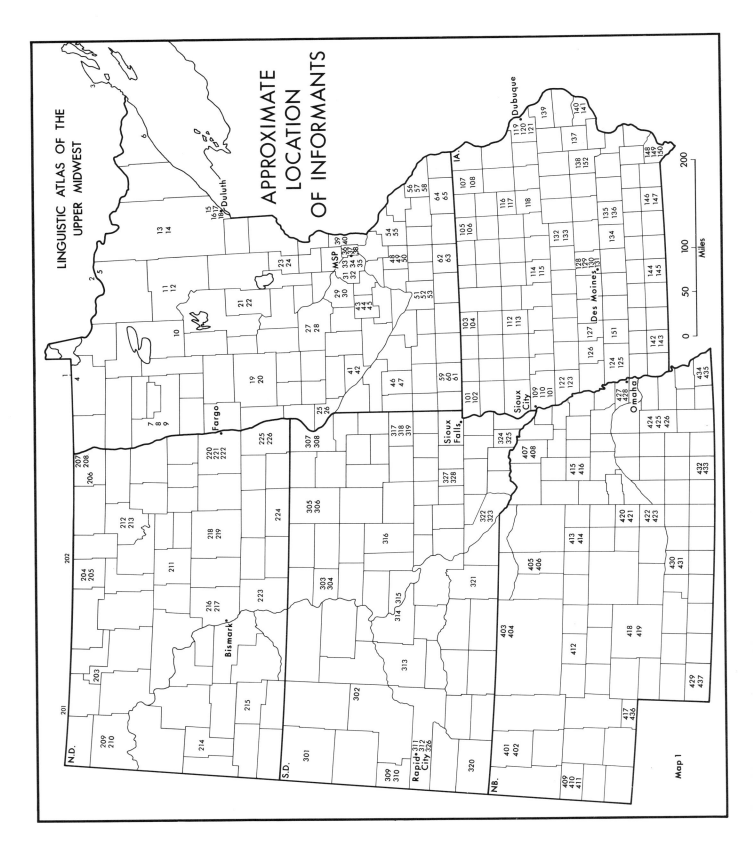

LINGUISTIC ATLAS OF THE
UPPER MIDWEST

APPROXIMATE
LOCATION
OF INFORMANTS

Map 1

6

PHONETIC SYMBOLS

Although Volume 3 will deal with pronunciation, for a few grammatical items the pronunciation is indicated in this volume where pertinent. The symbols used for this purpose are essentially those of the International Phonetic Association as slightly modified in 1930 for American dialect fieldwork, except that IPA [ɩ] here replaces American [ɪ] and that [ᵻ] replaces [ɨ]. A full description of the phonetic symolization may be consulted in Chapter 4 of *The Handbook of the Linguistic Geography of New England*.
Briefly, the vowel symbols are shown in the accepted vowel quadrilateral schema:

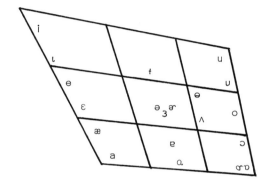

The consonant symbols are as follows:

stops	p t	tʃ	k	ʔ
	b d	dʒ	g	
fricatives	f θ s	ʃ		
	v ð z	ʒ		h
sonorants	m n l r		ŋ	
semivowels	w	j		

ABBREVIATIONS

A	Allen (fieldworker)
F	figure (= map)
fw.	fieldworker
G	Glenn (fieldworker)
H	Hanlin (fieldworker)
inf.	informant
M	McDavid (fieldworker)
NE	*Linguistic Atlas of New England*

occas.	occasional(ly)
P	Peterson (fieldworker)
UM	Upper Midwest
usu.	usual(ly)
VF	*A Survey of Verb Forms in the Eastern United States*
WG	*A Word Geography of the Eastern United States*
Wn	Wilson (fieldworker)
Wr	Weber (fieldworker)

RESPONSE LABELS

For a given variant the informants using it are identified by their serial numbers, separated by commas except when a semicolon indicates a state division.
One or several of the following symbols, nearly all of them identical with those used in the *Linguistic Atlas of New England* and described in the *Handbook of the Linguistic Geography of New England*, may precede an informant's number, with meaning as indicated below. A symbol preceding a series, e.g., †135-39, is relevant to all the numbers in the series, 135, 136, 137, 138, and 139.

c	spoken during conversation
cr	correction by informant
cvr	recorded conversational response
f	response forced by fieldworker
n	normal for informant
r	form repeated at fieldworker's request
s	suggested and normal for informant
vr	recorded on tape
:	hesitation on part of informant
!	amusement shown by informant
?	uncertainty on part of informant
ᴉ	heard in the community
†	archaic; old-fashioned
→	recently introduced; innovation
*	auxiliary informant
~	unchanged portion of repeated term

APPRECIATION

For this volume special appreciation is due to the editors of the University of Minnesota Press for pervasive help in the preparation of the manuscript for printing, and to Roberta Franklin for painstaking typing of the manuscript for offset printing.

CHAPTER 2

Verbs

TENSE FORMS

begin

73.6 He <u>began</u> to talk. NE 635. VF 6.

Because, as in the eastern states, most infs. respond with either <u>started</u> or <u>commenced</u>, the number offering a form of <u>begin is</u> too low to permit a comprehensive statement about the comparative frequency of the variants. (See Volume 1.)

More than three-fourths of the infs. who do use this term have the standard preterit <u>began</u>. In contexts of past time both <u>begin</u> and <u>begun</u>, particularly the former, are more likely to occur with Type I infs. <u>Begin</u> is so used by only one of the 11 Type II infs., but <u>begun</u> is used by four of them. Nine of the 11 Type II's choosing this lexical item rather than <u>start</u> or <u>commence</u> are in Midland speech territory, mostly in Iowa.

began /bi'gæn/ 4, 7-8, 11-12, 14, 22-24, 29-30, 32-33, c37, 39-40, 42, 46, 48-51, 54-55, 57-58, 61-63, 65; 104, 111-12, 115, 121-23, 129-31, 134, 136-38, 140-49, sn150; 206, 214-15, 217; 312, 318-19, 325-26; 401-2, c403, 408, 410, sn418, 419-21, 428, 433-35. /bi'gɛn/ 18; cvr126; 321; c414.

begin /bi'gɪn/ cvr107, c132; c315; 405, cvr427, c429.

begun /bi'gʌn/ s¹39, †40, c56, 64; c103, c105, 106, 108, 113, c116, c139; 409, cvr413.

bite

26.7 He was <u>bitten</u> (by a dog). NE 636. VF 6; F3.

As in the eastern states, the contrast between <u>bit</u> and <u>bitten</u> as past participle forms is essentially social rather than geographical. <u>Bit</u> is preferred by slightly more than one-half of the older and less-educated Type I infs.; <u>bitten</u>, by a higher proportion of Types II and III. But, perhaps as an effect of schooling in the more recently settled areas, it is also to be noted that the use of <u>bit</u> is less frequent in the three western states of the UM.

	Type I	Type II	Type III
bit	56%	21%	38%
bitten	45%	81%	68%

	Mn.	Ia.	N.D.	S.D.	Nb.	Ave.
bit	56%	45%	27%	43%	27%	39%
bitten	54%	55%	73%	57%	81%	62%

Two instances of South Midland <u>dogbit</u> occur: in the speech of a Type I inf. and of a Type II inf., both of them in southern Iowa just north of the Missouri border.

bit /bɪt/ 4, 6-7, 9, 13, 15-17, 19, 23, 25, 27, 31-32, 35-36, 38, 41, 43, 45, 50, c51, 52-53, c56, 58-60, 62-63; 101, 105, 107-9, 113, 115, 117-19, 124, 127, 129, 135-36, 139-41, 143, 146-47, 150-51; c204, 207, 212, 215-16, 220, 225; 302-3, 306-7, 311, 314-16, 319-20, 323, 327; 405, 407-8, c409, 415-17, 425, 429-30.

bitten /bɪtən/ 1-2, c3, 5, 8, 10-12, 14, 18, 20-22, 24, 26, 28-29, c30, 33-34, 37, 39-40, 42, 44, 46-49, c54, 55, 57, ?60, 61, ?62, 64-65; 102-4, 106, 110-12, 114, 116, 120-23, 125-26, 128, 130-34, 137-38, 144-45, 148-49, 152; 201-3, cr?204, 205-6, 208-11, 213-14, 217-19, 221-24, 226; 301, 304-5, 308-10, 312-13, 317-18, 321-22, 324-26, 328; 401-4, 406, 409-14, 416, 418-24, c425, 426-28, 431, sn432, 433-37.

dogbit 142, 145.

Comment:
<u>bit</u>: Inf. says 'bitten' because she wants to be correct; 'bit' is her ordinary term—60. "'Bit' or 'bitten'; I don't know which"—62. 'Bit' if "a dog bites once"; and 'bitten' if "more than one bite"—416. <u>bitten</u>: no 'dogbit'—431.

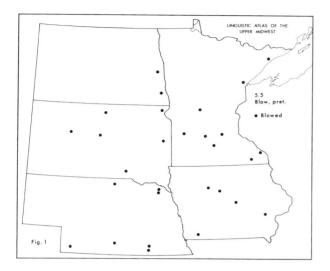

Fig. 1

blow

5.5 The wind <u>blew</u> hard. NE 637. VF 6, 38, 42.

Historical <u>blew</u> predominates in the UM as the preterit of <u>blow</u>. Analogical <u>blowed</u> is found in the speech of four out of five Type I infs. but in the speech of less than one-tenth of the Type II's. <u>Blowed</u> apparently is declining, since its incidence is much higher in most of the eastern states. Atwood found it in the speech of more than one-half of the Type I infs. in northern New England and of more than nine-tenths of those in North Carolina, although it is unusual in western New England, eastern New York, and eastern Pennsylvania.

No sharp Northern-Midland contrast is evident in the UM, where Minnesota's 14% frequency of <u>blowed</u> is only slightly higher than that in Iowa. But the decline of <u>blowed</u> is apparent even within the UM, since it is rare in the more recently settled regions of Minnesota and in the western third of the Dakotas and Nebraska. Like several others, this form seems to have suffered from attacks in the schools.

Inf. 220 also has <u>blowed</u> as participle.

blew 1-5, 7-15, 17-26, 28-34, 36-43, 45-50, 52-55, 57-60, 62-65; 101-13, 115-17, 119-31, cr?132, 133-37, 139-50, 152; 201-9, !210, 211-19, 221-26; 301, 304-6, 308-16, 318-21, 323-28; 401-2, c403, 404, 406, 408-25, 427-29, 431, 433-37.

blowed c6, 16, 27, c35, c42, 44, c51, 56, cvr64; c113, 114, 132, 138, 142; 220, c225; 302-3, 307, c314, 317, c322; c405, 407, c408, c429, 430, 432, c433.

no response 61; 118, 151; 426.

Comment:

  <u>blowed</u>: Corrected to 'blew' but inf. consistently uses 'blowed' in conversation.—132.

boil

37.2 <u>boiled</u> eggs. NE 294. VF 6.

In the UM <u>boiled</u> is the overwhelming choice as the participial adjective of <u>boil</u>. Three scattered instances of <u>boilt</u> appear in the speech of Type I infs. in northern Minnesota, northern North Dakota, and southern Nebraska. Statistically insignificant, these three nevertheless echo the conclusion of Atwood that <u>boilt</u> is distinctly a Type I usage in areas where the form itself is in the minority. Atwood's VF reports <u>boilt</u> as limited largely to the Midland speech area, but with a sprinkling of occurrences throughout the Middle and South Atlantic states excepting South Carolina and Georgia.

boiled /bɔild/ c1, 2-5, c6, 7-15, 17-22, !23, 24-50, c51-52, 53-58, c59, 60-61, c62, 63-65; 101-22, 124-41, 143, 146-50, 152; 201-5, 207-26; 301-4, 306-10, 312-26, c327, 328; 401-28, 430-37.

  boilt /bɔilt/ 16; 206; 429.

  no response 23; 142, 144-45, 151; 305, 311.

bring

22.4 I have <u>brought</u> your coat. NE 638. VF 7.

<u>Brought</u> is the well-nigh unanimous choice of UM infs. as the participial form of <u>bring</u> in the indicated context. Only four infs., two in Type I and two in Type II, have <u>brung</u>; and two others report having heard it in their communities. Its frequency is clearly much less than in the eastern states.

brought /brɔt/ c1, 2-3, 5-13, c15-18, 19-20, c21, 22-24, c25, 26-28, c29, 30, c31, f32, 33-34, c35, 36, 38, c39-40, 41, c42, f43, 44-45, c46-47, 48-49, c50, 51-55, s56, 57-60, c61, 62-65; 101-32, c133, 134-46, 148-52; 201-2, c203, 205-6, cvr207, 208-10, c211-12, 213, c214, 215-18, c219, 222-24, c225, 226; 301-5, *306, 307-15, 317-21, c322, 323-26, 328; 401-2, c403, 404, cvr406, 407-13, cvr414, 415-18, c419, 420-28, 430-33, s434, 435-37.

  brung /brʌŋ/ c15, ¹58, ¹65, *145, 147; 204.

no response 4, 14, 37; 204, 220-21; 316, 327; 405, 429.

Comment:
brought: "That doesn't sound right to me"—43. brung: "Said humorously only"—58. Inf. thinks this is "illiterate"—65.

buy

36.2 <u>boughten bread</u>. NE 285. VF 7.

Although apparently never used as a past participle instead of historical bought, the analogical English dialectal boughten gained early acceptance in the United States as a participial adjective, serving as an antonym for 'homemade.'

Boughten typically is heard in the context "bread," but its observed occurrence in several other contexts as illustrated below hints at a greater frequency than has been shown in only the responses to the question "What do you call bread that isn't baked at home?" for which a more usual reply is <u>baker's bread</u>. (See Volume 1.)

The UM distribution reflects that in the eastern states, particularly in New England, where there are reported 57 users of <u>boughten</u>, including cultivated speakers, in contrast to only two of bought. In the Middle Atlantic states the ratio shifts to 2:1. In the UM <u>boughten</u> is the choice of 56 infs., more than one-fourth of the total, who are consistently distributed by social class (26% of the Type I infs., 24% of the Type II's, and 25% of the Type III's) but not by area. Iowa and South Dakota have 37% and 39% respectively, while Minnesota has 20% and Nebraska only 14%. South Dakota has 23%.

Bought in this context is the choice of only three infs., two in Nebraska and one in Minnesota.

bought /bɔt/ 14; 425, 435.
boughten /bɔtən/ 4-5, c7, c22, 24, 26, 28, c36, 41, 43, 50, 56, ¹58, 63; 102, 106, 112-17, 127-28, 132-35, c137, 142-43, 145, 150; 205, 212, c214, 215, 220, 223; 302, 306-7, 310, c313, ¹318, 319, c323-24, c327, 328; 407, 411, 414, 429, 436.
Other instances of boughten: ~ one [not bread]—c327. ~ cookies—c22. ~ doughnuts—c214. ~ meat—c313. ~ bobsled—c323.

catch

74.2 Who <u>caught</u> it? NE 641. VF 8; F4.

The incidence of <u>catched</u> as the preterit of <u>catch</u> is much less in the UM than on the Atlantic coast. It occurs only six times in the UM in contrast with dominant caught. All infs. using it are in Type I and all, except one in southwestern Nebraska, are clustered in the area comprising central Minnesota and the eastern Dakotas.

catched /kɛtʃt/ 19, cvr25, c35; 220; 307; c417.
caught /kɔt/ All other infs., except that 118 and 151 did not respond to this item.

climb

69.7 He <u>climbed</u> up the tree. NE 642. VF 8; F5.

70.1 I've often <u>climbed</u> up a tree. NE 642. VF 8; F5.

The historical strong forms of <u>climb</u> persist almost as vigorously in the UM as in New England, where both preterit and participle were recorded, and in the Middle Atlantic states, where only the preterit was sought.

Although analogical <u>climbed</u> dominates in all types and in all five states, Midland <u>clum</u> is used as a preterit by one-half of the Type I speakers and one-third of the Type II speakers in Iowa, and it is not uncommon in Nebraska and South Dakota as well. As the past participle, clum is only slightly less frequent.

The preterit clim, characteristically Northern (although also with some occurrence along the South Atlantic coast), is consistently distributed in the UM with its relatively few occurrences in the older settlement areas of southern Minnesota, northern Iowa, and southeastern North Dakota. The participle clim, rarer, occurs within that same area—three times in southeastern Minnesota and once each in Iowa and North Dakota.

The three stray instances of <u>climb</u>, one as a preterit and two as a participle, may result from observation of imperfect articulation by the speaker, especially if he said "climb the tree" rather than "climb up the tree." It seems unlikely that <u>climb</u> here is analogous to the two instances Atwood noted in Black speech, where it presumably accords with rule-governed behavior that omits the preterit signal unless otherwise ambiguity would result.

Of the 55 infs. using strong verb forms nearly one-half consistently have the same form for both preterit and participle—24 with <u>clum</u> and five with <u>clim</u>. The others with a strong verb form have either clum or clim along with climbed.

Thirteen infs. using <u>clum</u> as the preterit have <u>climbed</u> as <u>the</u> participle;
seven who <u>use</u> <u>clum</u> as the participle
have <u>climbed</u> as <u>the</u> preterit. No inf.
has <u>both</u> <u>clum</u> and <u>clim</u>.

Preterit:

	Type I	Type II	Type III
clim	9%	1%	0
climbed	73%	86%	100%
clum	25%	12%	0

	Mn.	Ia.	N.D.	S.D.	Nb.	Ave.
clim	6%	8%	8%	0	0	5%
climbed	84%	65%	84%	96%	81%	81%
clum	9%	35%	8%	11%	22%	13%

   clim /klɪm/ 31-32, ¹40, 44, c55; 101,
104-5, 133; 220, 225.
   climb /klɑim/ 15.
   climbed /klɑimd/ 1-12, c13, 14, 16-20,
c23, 24-25, 28-30, 33-37, :38, 40-41,
c42, 43, 45-54, 56-58, 60-65; 102-3,
106-8, 110-11, 113-14, 116-17, 120-23,
125-26, :127, 128-31, 133-34, 136-37,
140-41, 143-44, 149-50; 201, !202, 203,
205-8, !209, 210-11, 213, c214, 215-19,
221-23, c224, 226; 301-21, 323-28; 402-3,
405-6, 408-13, 415, 417-23, c424-26, 427-
28, 430-36.
   clum /klʌm/ !¹10, 21-22, 26-27, ¹29,
c36, ¹40, ¹47, ?56, 59, ¹62, s¹65; 109,
112, c115, *116, 117, 119, 124, :127,
132, 135, 138-39, 142, 145-48; 204,
!¹210, 212; cr311, 316, c322; 401, sn403,
404, 407, 414, 416, 429, 437.
   no response 39; 118, 151-52.

Comment:
   <u>clum</u>: Used by inf.'s brother as a boy—
10. Inf. says this is used by boys—47,
62. Inf. uses 'clum' as third person
singular and 'climbed' as first person

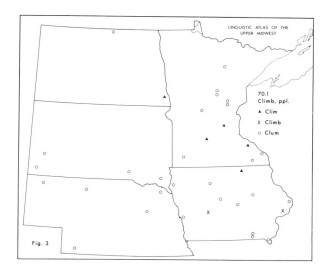

singular—117. Inf. says 'clum' is past
and 'climbed' is "more" present—311.

Participle:

	Type I	Type II	Type III
clim	4%	1%	0
climb	2%	0	0
climbed	76%	92%	100%
clum	23%	8%	0

	Mn.	Ia.	N.D.	S.D.	Nb.	Ave.
clim	5%	2%	4%	0	0	3%
climb	0	4%	0	0	0	...
climbed	86%	73%	92%	88%	89%	85%
clum	14%	22%	4%	16%	14%	15%

   clim 32, ?39, †40, 44, 55; 105; 225.
   climb 126, 140.
   climbed 1-12, c13, 14-20, 23, 25, :26,
28-31, 33-38, cr39, 40-43, ?44, 45-54,
57-58, 60-63, cr64, 65; 101-4, 106-8,
110-11, 113-14, 116-17, 119-23, :125,
127-31, 133-34, 136-38, 141-45, 149-50;
201-3, 205-13, c214, 215-24, 226; 302-5,
*306, 307, 309-15, 317-19, 321, 323, 325-
28; →401, 402-3, 405-6, 408-15, 417-28,
430-37.
   clum cr11, 21-24, 27, †40, ¹†45, 56,
59, 64; 109, 112, 115, 117, 124, 132,
135, 139, 146-48; 204, !¹215; 311, 320,
322, 324; 401, ¹403, 404, 407, 416, 429.
   no response 118, 151-52; 301, 308,
316.

Comment:
   <u>climbed</u>: Inf. thinks 'climbed' is her
usual form—11. "'Climbed' isn't right,
is it?"—44. "Now we say this"—64.

come

74.1 He <u>came</u> over to see me. NE 640.
VF 9.

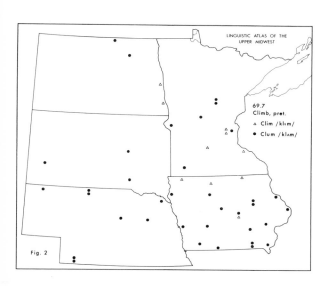

Despite school insistence upon the distinction between come and came, a high proportion of all infs. use come as a preterit instead of the prescribed came, some exclusively and others as the conversational and informal alternate. The general situation is hence like that reported by Atwood for New England and the Atlantic states.

The preterit come dominates among all UM Type I infs., three-fourths of whom use it. Four out of 10 Type II infs. have come, and two out of 10 Type III's. But, as the table below shows, two-thirds of Type I speakers also use came, as do four-fifths of Types II and III. For these infs. there seems, then, to be a live option, the choice being made in accord with the "register," the complex social context for a given utterance. Many infs. offered the fw. came in response to the question "If a man was at your house yesterday to see you, you'd say he did what in order to be there?" but freely used come in conversation.

No significant regional pattern is discernible in the UM. The slightly lower percentage of come in Iowa may be attributed to the less frequent recording of conversational items by the Iowa fws.

Infs. 30 and 209 also have came as participle.

	Type I	Type II	Type III
came	67%	89%	88%
come	75%	41%	19%

	Mn.	Ia.	N.D.	S.D.	Nb.	Ave.
came	80%	76%	81%	76%	78%	78%
come	60%	40%	50%	64%	67%	56%

came /kem/ c2, cvr3, c4, cvr5, cvr7-8, c9-11, cvrl2, c13, 14, c15, cvr16, c17, 18, c19, cvr20, c21, cvr23-24, 26, 28, c29-30, c32, 33, cvr37, c38, 39, c40, 41, c42-47, cvr49, c50-52, cvr53-55, c57-58, 59, c60-63, 64; 101-6, 108, 110-11, 113, 115-17, 119-21, 124, c125, 126-32, 134, 136-37, 139-41, 144-47, 149-50, 152; 201, c202-3, cvr204, 205, c206, cvr207, c210, cvr211, 212, c213, 214, c215, cvr216, 217, c219, cvr220, c221-22, 223, 226; 303-4, 306, c309, 310, c312, 313, c314, c317, 319, c320-21, cvr322, c323, 324-26, c327, 328; cvr402-3, c404, 406, 408-11, cvr413, 414, 416, c417, c419, 420-24, c425, 426-27, cvr428, c429, 430-32, c433, 435, 437.

come /kʌm/ c1, c3, cvr4-5, c6, c8, cvr12, c13, cvr15, c16, cvr17, c19, cvr21, c22-23, 24, c25, c27, c31, c34-36, cvr42, c43-48, c50, cvr51, c52, c54-55, 56, c57, s¹58, c59-60, c65; cvr104, c105, c107, c109, cvr112-13, 114, c115-16, 122, c123, 128, c133, c135, cvr138, c139, 140, 142-43, 148; c202-3, cvr204, cvr207-9, c210, c215, cvr216, c218, cvr220, c224-25; c301-2, 303, c*306, c309, cvr311, cvr314, c315, *316, cvr317, c320, cvr322, c323, c*324-25, cvr327; cvr401, c403-4, cvr405, cvr407, c408, cvr409, c412-14, cvr415, c416-17, cvr418, c419-20, cvr421-22, cvr427, cvr429, c430-32, c434, c436.

no response 118, 151; 305, 307-8, 318.

dive

69.5 He dived in. NE 580. VF 9; F6.

The UM incidence of the two preterit forms of dive strongly intimates that analogical English dialectal dove is becoming more widely accepted in preference to the historical dived.

As Atwood reports, dove had already become dominant in New England and New York State at the time of the eastern surveys. Dived has equal acceptance in the North Midland portion of Pennsylvania and is itself dominant elsewhere in the Middle Atlantic states. But a predictable majority use of dived in the Midland area of the UM is nonexistent. On the contrary, in nearly all of the territory dove is the more common form; in Minnesota and North Dakota, indeed, dove is dominant in a 3:1 ratio. Only in the strongly South Midland two southern tiers of counties in Iowa is dove unreported in the field data.

Despite the school textbook injunction against the use of dove in the first part of this century, the relative proportions of the two forms are not different among the three informant types. Both educated and uneducated speakers have approximately one-third dived and two-thirds dove.

The one instance of archaic div, a form described by Atwood as a minor variant in Type I speech in the South Atlantic region, comes from a Nebraska Type I inf. who has marked South Midland speech characteristics.

	Type I	Type II	Type III
dived	39%	30%	38%
dove	62%	72%	69%

	Mn.	Ia.	N.D.	S.D.	Nb.	Ave.
dived	32%	41%	19%	46%	32%	35%
dove	71%	61%	81%	54%	68%	67%

div /dɪv/ 429.

dived /daivd/ 1, 3-4, 14-16, 19, 25, c29, 30-31, 33, 35-36, 38-39, 43, 46-48, 52; 102, 104, ?107, 114, 117, 126-27, 131, 134-37, 140, 143-49, cr150; 202, 205-6, 213, 215; 303-4, 306, 308-9, 313, 317-18, 322, 324, 326-28; 403, 405, 410-12, 415, 421, 424, 426-28, 436.

dove /dov/ 2, 5-13, 15, 17-18, 20-24, 26-28, 32, 34, c35, 37, cr?39, 40-42, 44-45, !¹47, 49-51, 53-55, sn56, 57-63, *64, 65; 101, ?102, 103, 105-6, cr107, 108-13, 115-16, 119-25, 128-30, 132-33, 138-39, 141-42, 150; 201, 203-4, 207-10, c211, 212, 214, 216-26; 301-2, 305, 307, 310-12, 314-16, 319-21, 323, 325; 401-2, 404, 406-9, 413-14, 416-23, 425, 430-35, 437.

no response 118, 151-52.

Comment:
   dove: "A small boy might say this"—47. Usu.—150. "Another poor word"—312.

do

74.4 He did it last night. NE 690. VF 9.

In New England the preterit done is either the preferred choice of Type I and Type II speakers or, as in Massachusetts and Rhode Island, has at least fifty-fifty equality with did.

In the UM, however, factors which presumably include the influence of the schools have greatly reduced the preference for done. Only a slight majority of the less-educated infs. choose it, and it is offered by less than one-third of the high school group. But a number of the latter show some ambivalence, shifting from did to done and back again in the same social context.

No marked regional pattern appears, the slightly smaller proportion of done in Iowa apparently being due to fw. variation in recording conversational items.

Infs. 117, 212, and 403 also have did as participle in free conversation; and 317 has done as preterit.

	Type I	Type II	Type III
did	57%	81%	94%
done	63%	27%	6%

	Mn.	Ia.	N.D.	S.D.	Nb.	Ave.
did	72%	73%	69%	75%	60%	70%
done	43%	37%	42%	43%	51%	43%

did /dɪd/ 1-2, c3-4, c7, 8-10, c11, 13-14, c16, 17-18, 20, c21, 23-24, 28, c29, 30, 32-34, c36, 37-39, c40, c44-47, sn48, 49, c52-53, 54, cvr55, 57-59, c60-61, 62, c63, 64; 102-6, c107, 108, 110-11, c115, 116-17, 119-27, 129-31, 134, 136-37, 139, 141-42, 144-45, 148, 150, 152; 201-3, 205-8, 210-11, 213-14, 216, c217, 219, 221-23, 226; 302-5, *306, 309-10, c311-12, 313, 315, 318-21, 323-28; 402, 404, 406, 410-11, 413, 416, c417, c419, 420-21, c422, 424-26, 428, 430, 432-34, 437.

done /dʌn/ c3, 5, c6-7, c12, c15-16,

cvr19, c21, c22, !¹23, cvr25, 26, c27, cvr30, c31, c35-36, 41, c42-44, s¹48, c50-52, c56, 60, sn64, c65; c101, c104, cvr107, c109, c112-17, c132-33, c138, 140, 143, 146-47, 149; c201, cvr204, c207, c209, c212, c215-16, cvr218, c220, c224-25; c301-2, 306-8, cvr311, c314, 316, c317, c322, c*324, c325; c401, c404-5, cvr407, c408, cvr409, c414-15, c417-18, cvr423, c427, cvr429, cvr430-31, c434, 435, c436.
   no response 118, 128, 135, 151; 403, 412.

Comment:
   did: Used as past participle—c212; c420, cvr422.

dream

70.5 I dreamed all night. NE 643. VF 10.

The eastern over-all 2:1 ratio between dreamt and dreamed as preterits of dream persists in the UM with no appreciable regional variation except that the frequency of dreamt is somewhat lower in Nebraska. Nor is there any significant difference manifested among the three types of infs.

Variation does appear, however, with respect to the pronunciation of dreamt. The full consonant cluster with intrusive /p/ is more common in Northern speech territory, Minnesota and North Dakota. But /drɛmp/, with reduction of the cluster through loss of final /t/, is, along the Atlantic coast, more common among the Midland Type I speakers. In Iowa nearly one-third of the infs. have final /mp/;

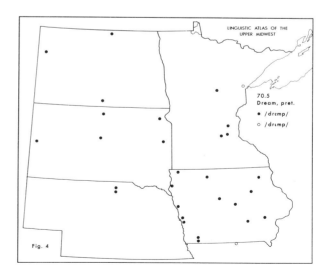

LINGUISTIC ATLAS OF THE UPPER MIDWEST

70.5
Dream, pret.
● /drɛmp/
○ /drɪmp/

Fig. 4

in all the states the Type I speakers are more likely than others to use this form.

Minor variants are /drɛmt/ and, once, /drʊmp/. The former is more likely to be used by a Midland Type III inf.

	Type I	Type II	Type III
dreamed	31%	34%	31%
dreamt	72%	71%	81%
/drɛmt/	5%	8%	19%
/drɛmpt/	46%	55%	56%
/drɛmp/	20%	8%	6%

	Mn.	Ia.	N.D.	S.D.	Nb.	Ave.
dreamed	32%	31%	23%	26%	46%	32%
dreamt	72%	76%	77%	82%	58%	72%
/drɛmt/	0	14%	0	19%	8%	7%
/drɛmpt/	65%	33%	65%	44%	43%	51%
/drɛmp/	6%	29%	12%	19%	5%	14%

dreamed /drimd/ 2, 10, c11, 12-14, 16, 22-23, 31, 33, cr?34, cr37, cr40, 45-46, 49-50, ¹53, c57, 59, 63, 65; 103, c107, 113-14, 120, 122, 126-27, 129, ?131, 133, 136, 141, 144-45, 148; 210-11, 213-14, ?215, 219, 226; 301, 304, 310, 313, 326-28; 401-2, c403, 404, 406, 411-13, 419, 423-24, 426-27, 429, 431-32, 434.

dreamt /drɛmt/ 117, 128, *145, 146-47, 149; 305-6, 316, 318-19; 425, c426, 430. /drɛmpt/ 1, 3-9, 15, 17-20, 24-30, 32, ?33, 34, 37, 39-44, ?45, 47-48, 51-56, 58, 60-62, 64, ¹65; 102, 105-6, c107, 110-12, 119, 121, 130, 133-34, 137, 139-40, 150; 201, c202, 203, 205-8, 212, cr215, 216-17, c218, 220-22, 224-25; 302, 310-12, ¹313, 315, 320-26; 407-10, 414-15, 417-18, 420-22, 428, 433, 435-37. /drɛmp/ 21, 35-36, 38; 101, 104, 108-9, 115-16, 123-25, 132, 135, 138, 142-43; 204, 209, 223; 303, 308, c309, 314, 317; 405-6. /drʊmp/ c16.

no response 118, 151-52; 307.

Comment:
dreamed: Usu.—310. dreamt: "I might say 'dreamt'"; inf. thinks it's a matter of euphony—33. "I say 'dreamt.' That's wrong, I know"—34. Usu.—37, 40.

drink

39.2 I drank a lot of it.
39.3 How much have you drunk? NE 644.
VF 10; F7.

Because of the long-continued usage controversy over the participial forms, the data for drink have received more than usual attention. See especially Walter S. Avis, "The past participle *drank*: Standard American English," *American Speech* 28(1953), 106-11, and Harold B.

Allen, "On accepting participial *drank*," *College English* 18(1957), 263-65. The controversy has centered upon the analogical replacement of the historical drunk by drank.

As the preterit, drank consistently is predominant from the East through the North Central states to the western limits of the UM. Two minor variants feebly survived the western migration. Analogical drinked, described by Atwood as frequent in northeastern New England and associated by Virginia McDavid with Kentucky and Ohio, is used by only two infs., a Type I southern Minnesotan of foreign-language background, and a Type II Iowan with New York and Pennsylvania grandparents. Drunk is used by two Type II's, a Minnesotan with a Maine background and a Nebraskan with parents from Maryland and Ohio.

The participle presents a quite different picture. Despite school influence for the acceptance of drunk, the dominance of drank over that form, observed in eastern and North Carolina I's and II's, is even stronger in the UM, where it not only is preferred by Types I and II but is even the usual form for nearly one-half of the cultured infs. as well. The 4:1 ratio for drank is remarkably consistent throughout the five states, although North Dakota and Nebraska show a somewhat smaller proportion of drunk.

Interest attaches to the modern development of the drank-drunk combination of preterit and participle in light of its inconsistency with the usual pattern exemplified by shrink and similar verbs. The Danish linguist Otto Jespersen suggested that the decline of historical drunk is due to its semantic association with intoxication. If so, then analysis of the data by sex might be significant, on the supposition that women are more sensitive to this association. In the UM not one Type I inf. using drunk is a woman. Of the male Type II's, 12% use drunk; of the female, 28%. Of the male Type III's, 60% use drunk; of the female, 40%. Female aversion to the term drunk can be inferred in the UM, then, only with respect to the uneducated.

Since virtually all the UM infs. use drank as preterit, the combination with drank as participle is by far the most common. The only inf. offering participial drunk who does not also have drank as the preterit is one with the leveled drunk-drunk pair of forms. Two infs. have drinked-drank, two have the reversed drunk-drank, and one has drank-drunken. These minor combinations occur in no clear regional patterns.

Preterit:
drank /dræŋk/ 1-12, c13, 14-39, 41-55,
57-65; 101-4, 106-49; 201-26; 301-6, 308-
28; 401-6, c407, 408-21, 423-27.
drinked /drɪŋkt/ c56; 105.
drunk /drʌŋk/ 40; !⊥†139; 422.
no response 150-52; 307.

Participle:

	Type I	Type II	Type III
drank	92%	78%	47%
drunk	8%	27%	60%

	Mn.	Ia.	N.D.	S.D.	Nb.	Ave.
drank	80%	81%	88%	78%	89%	83%
drunk	23%	25%	12%	22%	14%	20%

drank 1, 3-8, 10-12, 15-17, 19-27, 30-
32, 34, :35, 36-39, 41-43, 45-46, 48-53,
55-57, 59-64, !65; 101-6, 108-9, c112,
113-18, 120, c121, 122, :123, 124-25,
127-28, 130, :131, c132, 133-34, 137-40,
142-44, 146-49; 201-4, 207-21, 223-25,
⊥226; 301-3, c304, 305-6, 308-9, 311-12,
315-18, 320-21, :322, 323-25, 327; 401-5,
407-10, 412-18, 420-21, c422, 423, sn424,
?425, 426-30, sn431, 432-37.
drunk 2, 9, 13-14, 18, ⊥23, 28-29, 33,
40, 43-44, ⊥46, 47, 53-54, 58; 107, 110-
11, 119, 126, 128, 131, *134, 135, :!136,
141, 145; 205, 222, 226; 310, 313-14,
319, 326, 328; 406, 411, 419, 425, 431.
drunken ?425.
no response 129, 150-52; :?206; 307.

Comment:
drank: "I should say 'have drunk,' I
suppose"—34. "That's a peculiar expression, too"—65. "That sounds funny"—418.
Usu.—431. drunk: "A lot of people say
'drunk'"—23. "Bad English! 'Did you
drink' is correct English"—58. "I'm always conscious of using this"—411.

drive

9.8 I drove in a nail.
10.1 I have driven many a nail. NE 645.
VF 11; F8.

Standardization has been more effective
with the preterit of drive than with the
past participle.

As in the East, drove heavily dominates
in past-time contexts throughout the UM
but a much smaller proportion of minor
variants exists. Only five instances
occur in the UM, and then only as alternates for drove for two infs.

Driv /drɪv/, which has a better than
13% frequency in New England, mostly with
Type I and Type II infs., turns up only
twice in the UM, used by Type I farmers
in Minnesota and in Iowa. The Iowan then
corrected his reply to drove.

Druv /drʌv/, an uncommon variant reported by Atwood as found in northeastern
New England and in eastern Pennsylvania,
is used by two UM Type I speakers, one in
southern Minnesota of Ohio parentage and
one in Iowa of Illinois parentage.

Drived occurs once, in the speech of a
northern Minnesota Type I inf. whose
family language was Swedish.

Driven, as the past participle, competes with analogical drove both in the
East and in the UM, always with the highest incidence of drove among Type I infs.
In the UM no marked regional differences
appear except that drove is slightly less
frequent in Nebraska.

Both infs. who use driv as the preterit
have drove as the participle; the inf.
with drived as preterit has driven as the
participle; one of the infs. with druv
has driven as the participle and the
other has drove.

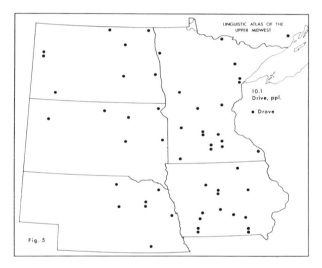

LINGUISTIC ATLAS OF THE
UPPER MIDWEST

10.1
Drive, ppl.
• Drove

Fig. 5

Preterit:
driv /drɪv/ c7; 113.
drived 4.
drove /drov/ 1-3, 5-8, :9, c10, 11,
c12-13, 14, c15, 16-18, c19-20, 21-25,
*26, :27, 28, c29, 30-41, c42, f43, c44,
45-46, c47, 48-58, 60-65; 101-12, cr113,
114-30, f131, 132-41, cr142, 143-52;
c201, 202-13, 215-26; 301-4, 306, c307,
308-10, c311, 312-15, 318, 320-26, c327,
328; f401, 402-18, c419, 420-21, c422,
423, c424, 425-28, cvr429-30, 431-37.
druv /drʌv/ 59; 142.
no response 214; 305, 316-17, 319.

Participle:

	Type I	Type II	Type III
driven	65%	90%	94%
drove	41%	13%	6%

	Mn.	Ia.	N.D.	S.D.	Nb.	Ave.
driven	74%	75%	81%	81%	86%	78%
drove	29%	27%	31%	23%	19%	26%

driven 1-2, 4, 6, 8-12, c13, 14, c17, 18, 20-23, 25-26, 28-31, c32, 33-34, 36-40, 42, 45-46, c47, 49, c52-53, 54-55, 57-59, 61-62, c63, 64-65; 101-4, 106-12, c113, 116, 118-26, 128-29, 131-33, 136-41, 144-45, 148-50, 152; 201-6, 208, 210-11, 213-17, 219, c221, 222-26; 301-2, 304, ?306, 308, c309-10, 311-15, cr316, f318, 319-21, c322, 323-26, 328; 401-4, 406, 408, c409-10, 411-12, c413, 414, 416-23, c424-25, 426, 428-31, 433-35, c436, 437.

drove 3-5, c7, c13, c15, 16, 19, 24, 27, ¹28, 35, †40, 41, 43, c44, 48, 50-52, 56, 60; 105, c113, 114-15, 117, 127, 130, 134-35, 142-43, 146-47, 151; c204, 207, 209-10, 212, c215, 218, 220; c301, 303, 306, 307, 316-17; !†401, 405, 407, c414, 415, c416, 427, 432.

no response 305, 327.

drown

69.6 He was <u>drowned</u>. NE 522. VF 12.

Regular <u>drowned</u> is the majority form for the past participle of <u>drown</u> in the speech of UM infs., although it competes with <u>drownded</u> among the less educated.

Nearly one-third of all Type I infs. use <u>drownded</u>, as do a few in Type II. No Type III speakers have it. Atwood's description of its distribution as heavier in Midland than in New York speech, and dominant in South Midland, is matched by the pattern in the UM, where the frequency is greater in Iowa than in Minnesota. However, it is well-nigh absent

from the more recently settled areas, that is, northern Minnesota and the western half of the Dakotas and Nebraska.

A variant <u>drown</u>, without the inflectional ending, is a rare minor form in Minnesota and Iowa. It may be due to overcorrection in the attempt to avoid the intrusive /d/ of <u>drownded</u>; it may be simply due to nonarticulation of the second member of this nasal + stop consonant cluster.

	Type I	Type II	Type III
drown	2%	6%	7%
drownded	29%	8%	0
drowned	71%	85%	93%

	Mn.	Ia.	N.D.	S.D.	Nb.	Ave.
drown	5%	10%	0	0	0	4%
drownded	11%	26%	12%	30%	14%	18%
drowned	86%	65%	88%	74%	85%	80%

drown /draun/ 14, 17, 60; 122-25, 133.

drowned /draund/ 1-4, 6-16, 18, 20-26, 28-34, 36-47, 49-55, 58, c59, 61-65; 101-8, cr?109, 110-11, cr?113, 115-16, 119-21, 126-32, 136-37, 141, 144-46, 148-50; 201-17, 219, 221-23, 225-26; 301-2, 304, 306, 308-14, 318-19, 321, 323-28; 402-14, 417-25, 427-29, 431-36.

drownded /draund+d/ c5, 19, 27, c35, ¹40, ¹42, 48, 56, c57; c109, 112, c113-14, 117, 134-35, 138, c139, 140, 142-43, 147; !¹215, c218, 220, 224; 303, 305, 307, c311, 316-17, 320, c322; 401, 415-16, ¹418, 430, c437.

no response 118, 151-52; 315; 426.

Comment:

<u>drownded</u>: "Children sometimes say 'drownded'"—40. Inf. says this is "incorrect"—418.

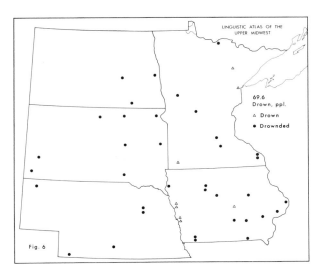

Fig. 6

LINGUISTIC ATLAS OF THE UPPER MIDWEST

69.6
Drown, ppl.
△ Drown
● Drownded

eat

38.5 We <u>ate</u> at six o'clock.
38.6 How often have you <u>eaten</u> today? NE 646. VF 12; F9.

Although standardization of <u>ate</u> as preterit and <u>eaten</u> as participle has progressed somewhat farther in the UM than in the East, both forms still undergo competition from variants, especially among Type I speakers.

The preterit <u>ate</u> /et/ is evenly predominant throughout the UM, with only a slightly lower incidence in Iowa than elsewhere. All Type III infs. have <u>ate</u>, nearly all the Type II's, and three-fourths of the Type I's.

The competition comes from simple <u>eat</u> /it/ and historical <u>et</u> /ɛt/. One-fifth of the Type I infs. use <u>eat</u>, largely in the southeastern quadrant of the UM,

16

that is, not in the most recently settled portions. Et occurs with somewhat lower frequency, chiefly in southeastern Iowa and the eastern Dakotas (note the accompanying map). It apparently has lost the older prestige status reported by Atwood as persisting in much of New England, since it is the choice of no Type I infs. and of only three Type II's, one each in Iowa and Minnesota besides one in Ontario. The use of et by this Canadian inf., whose father was born in England, probably reflects rather its status as the standard preterit in the United Kingdom.

With respect to the past participle, competition from the minor variants is so strong that in no state and in no type group does the frequency of eaten quite rise to that of the preterit ate. Ate itself is the main competitor, with a conspicuously even geographical spread of its 1:4 frequency among Type I infs. and 1:9 frequency among Type II's. Three of the five Canadian infs. have ate as the participle.

Nor, as the accompanying map shows, is there a marked regional pattern apparent in the distribution of the two other variants, eat and et, unless it be that the latter is less likely in the more recently settled areas, and, indeed, it occurs there only once in Nebraska and once in the Red River Valley of North Dakota.

As in the East, the common combination of the preterit-participle variants is standard ate-eaten. This is the preference of 136 of the 174 infs. responding with ate as preterit: 47 in Type I, 74 in Type II, and 15 (all) in Type III.

But, unlike the East, the UM has a

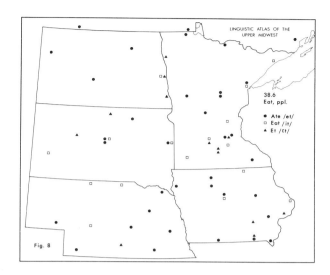

Fig. 8

fairly high proportion of users of the simple ate-ate pair, 30 out of 174, mostly Type I's. There are also 10 instances of the ate-eat combination (eight Type I and two Type II), and four of ate-et, split between Types I and II.

Preterit eat responses (19) occur mostly in the simple eat-eat pair (11) and in eat-eaten (nine), both, with one exception, from Type I infs. Eat-ate appears five times (four from Type I and one from II). The six et-eaten responses are divided equally between Types I and II, and et-ate appears once each in Type I and in Type II.

Preterit:

	Type I	Type II	Type III
ate	74%	97%	100%
eat	21%	3%	0
et	14%	3%	0

	Mn.	Ia.	N.D.	S.D.	Nb.	Ave.
ate	86%	81%	85%	85%	92%	86%
eat	13%	10%	8%	7%	19%	12%
et	8%	10%	12%	11%	3%	8%

ate /et/ 1, 3, c4, 5-6, 8-9, 11-12, c13, 14, c15-16, 17-20, c21, 22-24, 26-28, 30, 32-43, f44, 45-47, 49-50, f52-53, 54, c55, 56-58, c59, 60, c61-63, 64-65; 101-4, 106, c107, 108, 110, c111, 112-13, 115, c116, 117-31, 133-34, 136-38, 141-45, 148-49; 201-3, 205-13, cvr214, 215-19, 221-23, 226; 301-2, 304, 306, 308-10, c311, 312, c313, cvr314, 315, 317-21, 323-28; 402-3, c404, 406-8, c409-10, 411-16, c417, 418-26, 428-37.

et /ɛt/ 2, c7, c10, ⸸40, c51-52; c114, c135, 140, 146-47; c220, c224, 225; 303, 307, 316; 437.

eat /it/ c16, c25, c31, c44, c46, 48, c56, 59; c105, 109, c121, cvr132, c139;

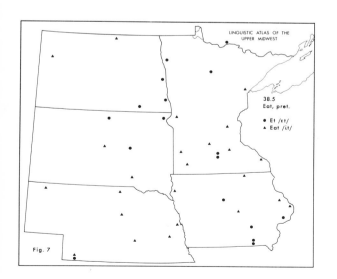

Fig. 7

38.5
Eat, pret.

• Et /ɛt/
▲ Eat /it/

204, cvr209; cvr314, c322; c401, 405,
c414, c422, 424, 427, c429.
no response 29; 150-52; 305.

Participle:

	Type I	Type II	Type III
ate	26%	11%	7%
eat	14%	2%	0
eaten	56%	88%	100%
et	11%	2%	0

	Mn.	Ia.	N.D.	S.D.	Nb.	Ave.
ate	18%	19%	15%	17%	19%	18%
eat	9%	6%	4%	13%	8%	8%
eaten	68%	68%	73%	79%	84%	73%
et	8%	6%	8%	8%	3%	7%

ate 1, 3-5, c15, 19, c21, 22, 27, 35,
c38, ¹58, 64; 104, 109, c112, 114, 117,
138, *145, 147, 149; 201, 209, c212, 216;
c306, c314, 315, c317; 407, 416-17,
c421, 424, 429, c432.
aten /etən/ ?113.
eat 6, c16, 31, c44, 48, c59; c105,
115, c139; 202, 220; 311, c314, c317;
c403, 405, c418.
eaten 2, 8-14, 17-18, 20, 23-26, 28-30,
c32, 33-34, 36-38, c39, 40-43, f44, !46,
47, 49-50, c53, 54-58, 60, c61, 62-63,
65; 101-3, 106-8, 110-11, 116, 118-19,
122-34, 136-37, 141-45, 148; c203, 204,
c205, 206-8, 210-11, 213-15, 217-19, 221-
24, 226; 301-2, 304, 306, 309, c310, 312-
13, 316, 318-21, 323-28; 401-4, 406, 408-
11, c412, 413, c414, 415, 418-28, 430-31,
433-37.
et cvr7, 35, ¹↑40, !45, c51, 52; 135,
140, 146; 220, c225; 302-3; c430.
no response 120-21, 150-52; 305, 307-8,
322.

Comment:
eat: Also said by inf.'s nine-year-old
son—117.

fight

75.6 They fought all the time. VF 14;
F10.

This item was added to the worksheets
after most of the Minnesota survey was
complete. The purpose was to ascertain
the extent to which South Midland fit had
been carried into the UM as the preterit
of fight.
Standard fought is well-nigh universal
among the infs. questioned. Only three
instances of fit appear. Two are in Iowa,
from a Type I inf. of Kentucky and Illinois parentage, and from a Type III
inf. of New York State parentage. One is
in eastern South Dakota, from a Type I
inf. both of whose parents came there
from Illinois.

fit /fɪt/ *122, 132; 316.
fought /fɔt/ c29, 30-31; 101-18, c120,
121-31, 133-35, 137-39, 141-50, 152; 215-
16, 220, 222, c223, 224-26; c301-2, 303-
5, 308, c309, 310-14, c315, f318, 319-26,
328; 401-2, c403, 404, c405, c407, 408-
11, c412, 413, c414, 415-16, c417-18,
419-35, c436, 437.
no response 1-28, 32-65; 136, 140, 151;
201-14, 217-19, 221; 306-7, 316-17, 327;
406, 424.

fit

22.5 His coat fitted me. NE 647. VF 14.

Besides the context given above, the
item was often sought by fw. A in the idi-
omatic expression "It fitted me to a T."
Although the eastern surveys clearly reveal the inflected preterit fitted as the
favored form in New England, with even a
fifty-fifty frequency in New York State,
and hence would predict its dominance in
much of the UM, the Midland simple fit
has so strongly expanded into Northern
speech territory that four out of five
of the infs. in all five states prefer
the latter.
The Northern provenience of fitted is
only dimly reflected in its somewhat
higher frequency in Minnesota and North
Dakota, and in its lowest frequency in
Nebraska, where four of the five infs.
with fitted have a German background and
the father of the fifth was born in New
York State.
Some school preference has existed for
fitted and is perhaps to be inferred from
the slightly higher, though statistically
insignificant, percentage of fitted among
cultivated speakers.
Three Type I infs., two in Minnesota
and one in North Dakota, admit vacillat-
ing between fit and fitted.

	Type I	Type II	Type III
fit	85%	84%	75%
fitted	18%	16%	25%

	Mn.	Ia.	N.D.	S.D.	Nb.	Ave.
fit	80%	86%	81%	85%	89%	84%
fitted	23%	14%	23%	15%	11%	17%

fit /fɪt/ 1-5, sn6, 8-13, 17-28, 30-32,
35-37, 39, ¹40, 41-45, ?46, cr*46, 47-51,
54-60, 62, 64-65; 101-2, 104-9, 112-25,
127-28, 130-39, 141-46, 148-51; 201,
c203, 204-8, 210-13, 215-18, 220-24, 226;
301-4, 306-12, c314, 315, 318-21, c322,
323-25, 327-28; 401-10, cr411, 412-14,
416-18, 420-23, 425-28, c429, 430, 432-
37.
fitted /fɪt+d/ cvr5, 7, 14-15, c16, 29,
33-34, 38, 40, cr46, 52-53, 61, 63; c103,

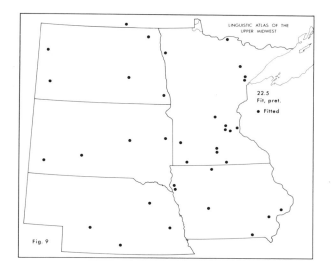

LINGUISTIC ATLAS OF THE
UPPER MIDWEST

22.5
Fit, pret.
• Fitted

Fig. 9

110-11, 126, 140, 147, 152; 202, 206,
209, 214, 219, 225; 313, *316, 317, 326;
?411, 415, 419, 424, 431.
  no response 129; 305.

Comment:
  fit: "It would be 'fit' with me. A
Swede would say 'fitted'"—6. "Improper"—
40.

freeze

6.5a The lake froze over last night. NE
648. VF 14-15; FII.

  With a single exception froze /froz/ is
the preterit form exclusively found in
the UM. The rare variant friz /frɪz/,
listed by Atwood as occurring in South
Midland areas, is used by one rural Iowa
Type II speaker (145) in South Midland
territory.
  Occasional recording of the past participle, especially by Iowa fws., yields
the supplementary contrast between 11 instances of frozen (64; 116, 123-24, 127,
132, 136, 139, 141; c415, 432) and eight
of froze (13, 59; c224; c303, 314; 407,
424, c435), the latter of which were recorded particularly because of their un-
usualness.

give

73.5 That's the one you gave me. NE
649. VF 15.

  Two forms appear as preterits of give
in the UM—historical gave and uninflected
give. Three-fourths or more of the infs.

in all five states typically say gave,
but in the folk speech of the Type I's
give retains strength. More than one-half
of the latter use give in contrast with
only one-fifth of the high school group.
Even three Type III speakers, however,
acknowledge occasional use of give as al-
ternative to their customary gave. Eastern gin and gived do not appear in the
UM data.
  Inf. 35 has give also as a participle.

	Type I	Type II	Type III
give	52%	19%	13%
gave	66%	94%	94%

	Mn.	Ia.	N.D.	S.D.	Nb.	Ave.
give	39%	31%	35%	32%	38%	35%
gave	74%	90%	77%	83%	76%	80%

  gave /gev/ 2-3, 5, 9-10, c11, 14,
cvr16, c17, 18-20, 22-24, 26-32, c33, 34,
36, c37, 38-40, 43, c44, 45-47, 49, c51,
52-55, 57-58, 60-65; 101-6, 108-16, 119-
27, 129-34, 136-38, 140-41, 143-50, 152;
201-3, 205-7, 209, c210, 211, 213, c214-
15, 216-19, 221-23, 226; 301, c302, 303-
6, cvr308, 309-10, 312-13, 315-19, c320,
321, 323-26, 328; 402, 406, 409, c410,
411, c412-14, 415-17, 419-21, 423-25,
c426, 427-28, 430-36, c437.
  give /gɪv/ c1, 4, c6-8, c12-13, c21,
c24-25, c27, 30-31, c35, †40, 41, c42,
c46, 48, 50, c51-52, c56, 59, c62; c104,
c107, c109, 115, 117, *122, 129-30, 133,
135, c139, 140, 142, 145, 148; c202,
c204, c207-8, c212, 216, cvr220, c224,
cvr225; c301, 307, cvr308, cvr311, c314,
320, cvr322, *324, c327; c401, c403-5,
c407-8, cvr415, c416, c418, c422, cvr423,
428, cvr429, 431.
  no response 15; 118, 128, 151.

Comment:
  give: Inf. uses 'gave' as participle—
c107.

grow

51.2 Bob grew a lot in one year.
51.3 You've grown big! NE 650. VF 15.

  As in the eastern states, each member
of the historical grew-grown preterit and
participle combination of grow is paral-
leled by analogical growed.
  Grew dominates in all five states, with
a social range from 72% among Type I
infs. to 100% among the cultivated.
Growed, sometimes used with grew by the
same speaker, correspondingly has about a
one-fifth frequency in all states,
slightly more in South Dakota, with a 3:7
ratio among the Type I infs.
  Grown likewise dominates as the parti-

19

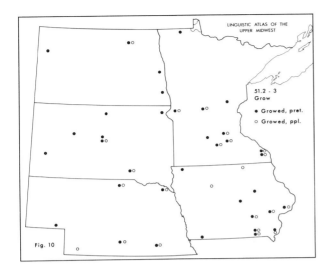

cipial choice in all five states, but with even greater strength than growed. Only 16% of the uneducated speakers use growed, least often in the two Dakotas.

Slightly more than one-half of the infs. with the preterit growed also have growed as the participle; most of these are in Type I. Less than one-half have grown; 88% are in Type I. Grew-growed is the combination favored by four Type II infs. and two Type I's. One Type I Iowan has the combination grew-grew.

Preterit:

	Type I	Type II	Type III
grew	72%	93%	100%
growed	28%	8%	0

	Mn.	Ia.	N.D.	S.D.	Nb.	Ave.
grew	86%	80%	85%	76%	87%	83%
growed	14%	20%	15%	28%	13%	17%

grew /gru/ 1-3, 5-14, c15, 16, c17, 18-22, c23, 24, 26, 28-29, cvr30, 31-34, 36-43, :f44, 46, c47, 49-50, 52-55, c57, 58-65; 102-6, sn107, 108-16, 118-31, 133-34, 136-37, sn139, 141-42, 144-45, 149-50, :152; 201-8, 210-11, 213-19, 221-24, 226; 301, 304, 306, 309-10, 312-14, 316, 318-21, 323-28; 401-2, c403, 404, 406, 408-16, c417, 418-20, c421, 422-23, c424, 425-29, 431, 433-35, 437.

growed /grod/ 4, c25, 27, c35, ¹39, !45, 48, c51, 56, c57; 101, 117, c132, 135, 138, 140, 143, 146-47, c148; 209, c212, 220, c225; 302-3, 307, 311, c314, 315, c322; 405, 407, 430, c432, c436.

no response 151; 305, 308, 317.

Comment:
grew: "That don't hardly sound right"—44. growed: "Improper"—39.

Participle:

	Type I	Type II	Type III
growed	16%	9%	0
grown	84%	94%	100%

	Mn.	Ia.	N.D.	S.D.	Nb.	Ave.
growed	12%	16%	4%	7%	14%	12%
grown	88%	88%	96%	93%	89%	90%

grew /gru/ 109.
growed /grod/ 24-25, 27, c35, ¹39, 48, c51, 56, c57; c105, c113, 135, 138, 140, 146-47, c149; 212; 315, c322; 405, 407, c429, 430, 432.

grown /gron/ 1-14, c15, 16-17, c18, *19, 20-21, c22, 23, 26, 28-34, 36-47, 49-50, 52-55, 58-60, cvr61, 62-65; 101-8, 110-12, 114-34, 136-39, 141-45, 148-50, 152; 201-11, 213-18, c219, 220-21, c222, 223-26; 301-7, 309-14, 316-21, 323-28; 401-2, c403, 404, 406, 408-24, c425, 426-29, 431, 433-37.

no response 151; 308.

hear

10.6 I have heard it. NE 633. VF 16.

The consistent dominance of participial heard in New England and eastern Pennsylvania is duplicated in the UM, where the only variant, heared, turns up three times from Type I infs. in South Dakota and Nebraska. South Midland heern apparently could not withstand midwestern winters.

heard /hɚd/ All other responses.
heared /hɪrd/ c322; c403, 429.
no response 12, 21, 31, 37-38, 50; 106, 117-18, 128, 131, 135, 142, 151; 201, 203, 205, 208, 215-16, 222-24, 226; 306, 313, 316-18, 321, 328; 408-9, 413, 415, 419-22, 424, 428, 432, 434-35.

heat

40.1 Heated up (of food). NE 313. VF 16.

Because of the common use of synonymous warmed up and warmed over (see Volume 1), only nine instances of the word heat appear in the responses to the query about this item. Seven of these are of the standard heated, and two, both from Type I speakers in South Dakota and Nebraska, are of het /hɛt/, a variant frequent in northeastern New England and sporadic elsewhere in the East.

In other contexts, however, het occurs as participle in the free conversation of infs. 105, 109, 112, and 316, and as preterit in the free conversation of 114, 311, and 404.

heated /hit+d/ 14, 18, 52, 58; 120-21; 426.

het /hɛt/ 135; 311.

kneel

70.2 She <u>kneeled</u> down. NE 652. VF 17.

The eastern dominant position of <u>knelt</u> as the preterit of <u>kneel</u> is more than matched in the UM, <u>where</u> it is the choice of four out of five infs. Its regional spread is fairly even, with only a slightly lower incidence in South Dakota and Nebraska.

Correspondingly, the variant <u>kneeled</u>, which is used by one-third of the <u>New</u> England infs. irrespective of types and by about one-fourth of those in the Middle Atlantic states, retains popularity among UM Type I speakers but, perhaps because of school influence, is much less common among the better educated.

	Type I	Type II	Type III
kneeled	30%	17%	13%
knelt	73%	84%	88%

	Mn.	Ia.	N.D.	S.D.	Nb.	Ave.
kneeled	21%	16%	23%	29%	30%	23%
knelt	82%	84%	81%	71%	72%	79%

kneeled /niⁱld/ 4, 13-14, 19, 21-23, 29, 31, 35, 48, 52, 57, 63; 101, 107, 113, 116, 135-36, 140, 143; *202, 207, 220-22, 226; 304, 307-8, 311, 314-16, 327; :405, 412, 415, 423, 425, 427, 429, 432-33, c434, 437.

knelt /nɛlt/ 1-3, 5-10, c11, 12, 15-18, 20, 24-28, c29, 30, 32-34, :36, 37-47, *48, 49-51, 53-56, 58-62, 64-65; 102-6, 108-12, 114-15, 117, 119-34, 137-39, 141-42, 144-50; 201-6, 208-16, :217, 218-19, 223-25; 301-3, 305-6, 309-10, 312-13, ¹314-15, 317-26, 328; 401-2, 404, 406-11, 413-14, 416-22, 424, 426, 428, 430-31, 434-36.

no response 118, 151-52; 403.

learn

73.2 Who <u>taught</u> you that? NE 666. VF 17.

In the context given above 12% of the UM infs. respond with a preterit form of <u>learn</u> instead of <u>teach</u>. (See Volume 1.) Most of these, a <u>total</u> of 60, are in Type I, with an even balance of those favoring <u>learned</u> and those favoring <u>learnt</u>. Although Atwood found a trend <u>toward</u> <u>learned</u>, the UM shift seems to be toward <u>learnt</u>, which indeed is the choice of four of the five Type II speakers using

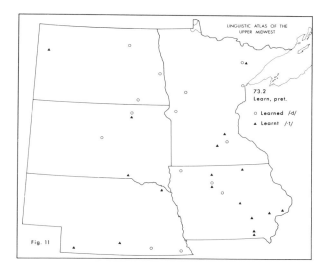

Fig. 11

<u>learn</u> instead of <u>teach</u>. Cultivated infs. have only <u>teach</u> in this context.

No marked regional contrasts appear except that <u>learnt</u> is proportionately more likely to occur in Iowa than in the other states.

learn /lɜn/ c25.

learned /lɜnd/ c13, 17, 19, !¹21, 25, †40, 48; 101, c112, 114, 142; 212, 220, 224; cvr305, c314; 432, 434.

learnt /lɜnt/ c13, 35, 44, c51; 104, c105, c113, c132, 135, 138, 140, 146-47; 209; 306, c322; 407, 429-30.

lie

70.3 I'm going to <u>lie</u> down.
70.4 He <u>lay</u> in bed all day. NE 494, 653. VF 18.

Despite the long-continued prescriptive influence of the schools, the historical relationship between <u>lie</u> and <u>lay</u> retains vitality only in the <u>persistence</u> of <u>lie</u> as a present form among fairly well educated speakers. With the preterit <u>lay</u> the older distinction survives with difficulty.

As in the eastern regions, in the given context the infinitive <u>lie</u> holds only a firm two-thirds majority position in the UM, with a somewhat larger margin of frequency in Iowa. One-half of the Type I's use <u>lay</u> in this context, nearly half of the Type II speakers and even two out of 10 of the college graduates. Several infs., though none in Type III, evidence confusion by shifting uncertainly from one form to the other.

The analogical preterit <u>laid</u>, probably confused also with the preterit of the related verb lay, is the choice of three-fourths of the Type I speakers, two-thirds of the Type II's, and, in defiance of "grammar rules," nearly one-half of the college graduates. Minnesotans apparently are most bemused by the lie/lay distinction, South Dakotans least. Historically "correct" lay is the response of only 16% of the Minnesota infs. but of just one-third of the South Dakotans; 15% of the Type I infs. use it, more than one-fourth of the Type II's, and a bare majority of the cultivated speakers.

The form lied provides a solution to this grammatical Scylla and Charybdis for 13% of the South Dakotans and for a scattered few elsewhere—all in Types I and II. Three Type I infs.—one in Minnesota and two in Iowa—warily shun any inflected forms and cling to simple lie as their choice for preterit.

These variations for the morphological slots allow for several present-preterit combinations. Most common of these is lie-laid. One-half of the Type III infs. do have the school-fostered lie-lay combination, but only 17 Type II infs. use it, and only 10 in Type I. Of those offering lay as the present infinitive, about three-fourths have the preterit laid. Other less frequently occurring combinations are lay-lay (five Type I's and nine II's), lie-lied (four Type I's and two II's), lie-lie (two Type II's), and lay-lie (a single Type I).

Present Infinitive:

	Type I	Type II	Type III
lie	60%	70%	81%
lay	52%	40%	19%

	Mn.	Ia.	N.D.	S.D.	Nb.	Ave.
lie	65%	73%	58%	68%	64%	66%
lay	48%	32%	46%	46%	53%	45%

lay /le/ 4-5, c6, 7, c8-9, 11-12, c13, c15, c19, c21-23, c29-32, c35, 36, 38, c42-44, c48, c51, 52-53, sn56, 60, c63; c107, 109, 117, 119, c120, 123, 125, 130, 132, 135, 140, 143, 146-47, 149; c202-3, 206, c209, c212, c218-21, c223-25; 301-4, ?*306, 307-8, c311, 314, c315, c320, 322, c323, c327; c401, c403, c405-8, c410, 413, cvr414, 416-17, c419, 421, c423, c429, cvr430, 431, c432, 435.

lie /laɪ/ 1-3, 8, 10-11, 14, 16-18, 20, 22, 24-28, 30-32, c33, 34-35, 37, 39-41, cr?42, 44-47, 49-50, 54-55, 57-59, ?60, 61-62, 64-65; 101-8, 110-16, 120-22, 124, 126-29, 131, 133-34, 136-39, 141-42, 144-45, 148, 150; 201, 204-5, 207-8, 210-11, 213-17, 222, c224, 226; 302, 305, cr*306, 309-10, 312-13, c315, 316-21, 324-28; 402, 404, c405, 408, c409, 410-15, 418, 420, 422, 424, c425, 426-28, 432-34, 437.

no response 118, 151-52; 436.

Comment:
lay: "Should be 'lie down,' shouldn't it?"—38. Inf.'s usage, but she thinks 'lie' is "right"—60. lie: "I'd never say 'lay down'"—404.

Preterit:

	Type I	Type II	Type III
laid	77%	69%	47%
lay	15%	28%	53%
lie	3%	0	0
lied	6%	4%	0

	Mn.	Ia.	N.D.	S.D.	Nb.	Ave.
laid	81%	72%	65%	54%	68%	71%
lay	16%	21%	27%	33%	29%	23%
lie	2%	4%	0	0	0	2%

laid /led/ :f1, 2-3, c5, 6-13, cvr15-16, c19, 21-22, c24, c25, 26-28, c29, c31, 35, 37-45, 47, s48, 49, c50, 51-53, c54-55, 56-62, c63, 64; 101-5, 107-9, 111, 114-15, :116, 117, 119, 121, 123, 125, 128-30, 133-35, 137-39, 141, 143-49; 203, c204, 205, c206, cr207, 208-10, c211, cr212, 215, cvr216, 218-19, 223-24, c225; 304, 306-7, 309, 312, cvr314, 315-16, cvr317, 319-20, c322, 324; 401-4, cvr407, c408, 411-13, 415-16, 418, c419, 423-24, 426-27, c429, 432-34, 436-37.

lay /le/ 14, 16, 18, 20, 32-34, 46, c48, 65; 106, 110, 112, 120, 124, 126-27, 131, 136, 150; 202, 213-14, cvr217, c221-22, 226; c303, 308, 310, c311, 325-28; 406, 410, c414, 420, 422, 425, 428, 430-31, 435.

lie /laɪ/ 55; 113, 132.

lied /laɪd/ 4, 23; 142; 201, ?207, ?212, 220; 318, 321, 323; 409.

no response 17, 30, 36; 118, 122, 140, 151-52; 301-2, 305, 313; 405, 417, 421.

Comment:
laid: Inf. says 'lay' and 'lie' confuse her—2.

might

75.7 I might be able to. VF 18; F14.

After the completion of the Minnesota portion of the study this item was added to the worksheets in order to ascertain whether South Midland mought had been carried into Iowa and Nebraska. Only might, however, appears in the field records.

ride

27.7 I have never ridden a horse. NE 655. VF 19; F15.

Ridden is the participial choice of most UM infs., but its dominance has been strongly threatened by rode.

Although the eastern distribution pattern revealing rode as Midland-oriented is perhaps reflected in its concentration in the southern half of Iowa, the more conspicuous UM contrast is between the eastern and the western states of the area. Like some other grammatical items subject to school attention, rode, as a form categorized unfavorably in the classroom, is less frequent in Nebraska and the Dakotas, the more recently settled part of the region.

As in the East, rode is much more heavily favored by Type I speakers, for whom it is the dominant form in each state but South Dakota. The effect of the schools may appear in the rather wide difference between its 59% for Type I and only 21% for Type II, with a somewhat surprising incidence of 19% among the better educated speakers.

One result of the confusion caused by the competition of ridden and rode may exist in the speech of an Iowa Type I inf. (112), who apparently has solved the conflict to his own satisfaction by assigning the contrast to the number of the verb object. "I've rode a horse," he said, but "I've ridden horses."

Archaic rid, found sporadically in northeastern New England and in the South Midland, is reported only once, in the speech of a Type I South Dakotan whose father was born in Vermont.

	Type I	Type II	Type III
ridden	48%	82%	81%
rode	59%	21%	19%

	Mn.	Ia.	N.D.	S.D.	Nb.	Ave.
ridden	58%	58%	73%	78%	72%	65%
rode	48%	48%	35%	22%	30%	39%

rid /rɪd/ cvr317.
ridden /rɪdən/ 1-4, 8-10, 12-14, 18, 20-22, ?24, 25-26, 28, c29, 31, c33, 36-39, 42, 44, 46-47, 49, 54-55, 57, 60-65; 101-4, c105, 107-8, 110-11, c112, 113, 116, 119-24, 126-28, 130-31, ?132, 136-37, 144-45, 149-50, 152; c201, 202-5, 208-11, 213-15, 217-19, 221-23, c226; 301, ?302, 304, 307-10, 312-13, 315-24, c325, 326, 328; 401-4, 406, 408-10, c411, 412-13, 418-20, 422-23, 425-26, 428, 430-31, 433-37.
rode /rod/ c5-6, 7, 11, 15-17, 19, 23-24, 27, 30, 32, 34-35, c36, 40-41, 43, 45-46, 48, 50-53, 56, 58-59, c60, †62, 63; c105, 106, c109, c112, 114-15, c116, 117-18, 125, 129, cr132, 133-35, 138-43, 146-48, 151; c204, 206-7, c209, 212, 216, 220, 224-25; cr302, 303, 305-6, 311,

314; †401, 405, 407, c414, 415-17, 421, 427, cvr429, 432, c434.
no response 327; 424.

Comment:
rode: "I suppose I should have said 'ridden'"—24. "Most of them say 'rode'"—62.

rise

4.1 The sun rose at (six). NE 657. VF 19; F16.

Comparative frequencies for the preterit of rise would be misleading, since in the context given above, it alternates as a lexical response with come up. (See Volume 1.) Of the infs. replying with the verb rise 90% use the standard preterit rose. Raised, a Midland variant, is briefly scattered among Type I speakers in Minnesota, Iowa, and South Dakota. Rised, also a minor Midland form found in Ohio and Kentucky, occurs in the speech of four Type I infs. in Minnesota and South Dakota, two of whom have foreign-language background and two of whom have Ohio parentage.

raised /rezd/ cvr4, c6, 25; c132, 142; 306-7.
rised /raɪzd/ 4, 19, 35; 303.
rose /roz/ 1-3, 5-12, 14-15, 17-18, 20-24, 26-31, c32, 33-34, :36, 37-38, 40-47, s48, 49-58, 60, 62-65; 101-12, 114, 117, 119-27, 129-31, 133, 135-38, 140-41, 143-44, 147-50, 152; 201, 203-6, :207, 208-14, 216-22, f223, 224-26; 301-2, 304-5, 308, 310, 312-20, 324-28; 401-2, 404, 407, 411-16, 418, 420, 422, c423, 425-28, 430-33, 435-37.

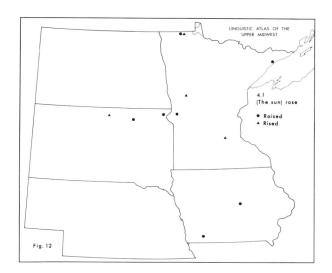

LINGUISTIC ATLAS OF THE UPPER MIDWEST

4.1
(The sun) rose

● Raised
▲ Rised

Fig. 12

23

come or no response 13, 16, 39, 59, 61;
113, 115-16, 118, 128, 134, 139, 145-46,
151; 202, 215; 309, 311, 321-23; 403,
405-6, 408-10, 417, 419, 421, 424, 429,
434.

run

73.7 He ran. NE 658. VF 20.

With respect to the third-person singular preterit, the conflict between the
school insistence upon historical ran and
the powerful leveling tendency toward use
of analogical run has led a rather high
proportion of speakers to be uncertain
about which form is "correct."

Of the Type I's 30% vacillate between
one form and the other, as do 26% of the
Type II's; even 26% of the college group
use both forms. But it still is evident
that the significant contrast between
ran and run in a past context is primarily social, not regional. All the college-
type speakers use ran at least part of
the time, as do most of the high school
group and two-thirds of the least educated. But two-thirds of the least educated
also use run, and so do one-third of the
Type II's, but only one-fifth of the Type
III's. Run as preterit thus connotes both
lack of formal education and extreme conversational informality, sometimes only
the second. Among all types the evidence
for the use of run is found primarily in
free conversation.

Perhaps a slight regional difference
is to be found in the fact that only in
southern Iowa, South Dakota, and Nebraska
do the Type I infs. generally prefer run.

	Type I	Type II	Type III
ran	63%	90%	100%
run	65%	36%	19%

	Mn.	Ia.	N.D.	S.D.	Nb.	Ave.
ran	86%	76%	81%	68%	67%	77%
run	46%	37%	54%	71%	51%	49%

ran /ræn/ 2-3, 5-12, c13-15, 17-18, 20,
22-28, c29, 30, 32-34, 36-41, 43, 45-50,
c51, 52-54, c55, 57-65; 101-4, 106, 108,
110-11, 113-15, 118-24, c125, 126-27,
129-32, 134, 136-38, 141-45, f146, 147,
149-52; 201, c202-3, 204-8, 210-11, c213-
14, 215-17, c218, 219, 221-23, c225; 301-
4, cr?305, 307, 309-10, 313, 315-16, 318-
19, 321, 323, c324, 325-28; 406, 410-14,
416, 418-28, 430-36.

run /rʌn/ 1, c4, 6, c8, c13, c15-16,
17, c19-20, 21, c23, c25, c29, c31, c34-
35, c38, 39, c40, 41, c42, 44, c46, c48,
c51, 53, c56, 59, c65; c102-3, c105,.
c107, c109, 112, cvr113, c115-16, 117,
c121, cvr132, c133, 135, c139, 140, 145,

c146, 148; c203-4, c209, 210, c212, 215-
16, c218, c220, 221, c223-26; 301-3, 305-
6, cvr308, 309, c311-12, c314-15, c317,
*318, cvr320, 321, c322, 323, c324-25,
cvr327; cvr401, c402-5, cvr407, 408,
c409, c414, 415, cvr416, c417, 421, c422,
423, cvr427, cvr429, c436-37.

no response 128.

scare

56.5 I'm scared. NE 475.

Approximately 80% (161) of all infs.
responded to this lexical item with the
word scared. (See Volume 1 for afraid,
frightened, etc.) Of these infs., evenly distributed among the five states,
three-fourths use the pronunciation
scared /skɛrd/ and one-fourth use the
pronunciation scairt /skɛrt/.

Minnesota has the highest incidence
of scared and North Dakota the lowest,
a distribution that does not conform with
the usual Midland-Northern contrast.
Scairt, though found in all five states,
is not reported in the most recently settled areas, i.e., the western fringe and
northern Minnesota. Consistent with this
characteristic of a recessive grammatical
form in the UM is its greatest frequency
among Type I speakers. Only two Type I
infs. have scairt, both of them in
Minnesota.

The following percentages are of the
infs. offering scared, not of the total
number of UM infs. replying to the query.

	Type I	Type II	Type III
scairt	29%	22%	18%
scared	77%	77%	82%

	Mn.	Ia.	N.D.	S.D.	Nb.	Ave.
scairt	20%	23%	38%	27%	27%	25%
scared	82%	79%	67%	77%	77%	78%

scairt /skɛrt/ 24, 31, 34, c35, c44,
sn49, 50, 57, c64; c105, 112-13, 117,
121, c124, 138, 140, 143, 149; :208,
c209, 212, 216-17, c219, c223, 225; c302-
3, c304, 306, c317, c327; c403, c407,
sn415, 416, 427, c430, 434, 437.

scared /skɛrd/ 1, 4, c5, 6-10, c11, 12,
14, c15-16, c19, 20, c21, :22, s23, c25,
26-30, 33, c35, 36-37, 39, 42-43, 45-48,
52, 56, 58; 101-11, 114-16, 119-20, 122,
124-25, 127-30, c132, 133-34, 136-37,
141-42, 144-46, 148; 201-2, 204-5, 209-
10, 213-15, 218, c220, 222, 224; c303,
305, 307-8, sn310, :311, c312, 313, !314,
315-16, 318-21, 325-26, 328; 402, cvr403,
408-9, †410, 411-12, c414, c417, 418-21,
c422, 424, c425, 426, 428, c429, 431-33,
435-36. a-scared 123.

other or no response 2-3, 13, 17-18,

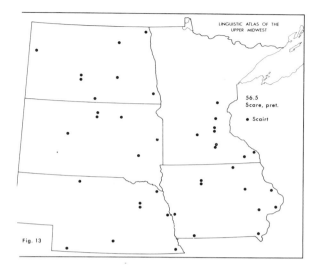

Fig. 13

32, 38, 40-41, 51, 53-55, 59-63, 65;
118, 126, 131, 135, 139, 147, 150-52;
203, 206-7, 211, 221, 226; 301, 309,
322-24; 401-2, 404-6, 413, 423.

see

74.2 He <u>saw</u> me. NE 659. VF 20; F17.

Standard <u>saw</u> is the dominant preterit
of <u>see</u> among the three informant types
in all five states, with greatest frequency in Type III. Eastern regional
variants <u>see</u>, <u>seed</u>, and <u>seen</u> also occur,
chiefly in use by less-educated speakers.

<u>See</u>, common as a preterit in New Eng-
land and found as well in Virginia and
North Carolina, survives in the UM. It
is scattered in the older part of Northern territory, except for its use by two
Nebraska infs., one with a Wisconsin
father and one with an Iowa mother.

<u>Seed</u>, a South Midland variant, occurs
only in the speech of two Type II infs.,
one South Dakotan and one Nebraskan,
neither of them with immediate South Midland ancestry.

<u>Seen</u>, typically Midland in the Atlantic
states, has extended its range to cover
also the Northern speech territory of
Minnesota and North Dakota.

The standardizing influence of the
schools may be the cause of the uncertainty several infs. manifest: 21% of
the Type I speakers alternate between
<u>saw</u> and <u>seen</u>, as do 12% of the Type II's.
Three Type I's use both <u>saw</u> and <u>see</u>. Two
infs., a II and a III, alternate between
<u>see</u> and <u>seen</u>.

<u>Saw</u> also occurs as the participle in the

conversation of infs. 42, 311, 321, and
401.

	Type I	Type II	Type III
saw	73%	82%	87%
see	13%	1%	7%
seen	42%	27%	13%

	Mn.	Ia.	N.D.	S.D.	Nb.	Ave.
saw	86%	72%	80%	67%	79%	78%
see	6%	6%	8%	15%	6%	8%
seen	34%	38%	28%	44%	21%	35%

saw /sɔ/ c1, 2, c3, 4, c7, 9-12, c13,
14, c15, 16-18, c19, 20-21, c22, 23-24,
26-28, c29-30, 31-32, c33, 34, c35, 37-41,
c42, 43, c44, 45, c46-47, 49, cvr51, 52-
55, 58, c59, 60, c61-63, 65; 102-4, 106,
110-11, 114, 116-17, 119-21, 123-24, c125,
126-31, c132, 133-34, 136-41, 144, 146-48,
150, 152; 201-2, c203, 205-8, 210-11, 213,
cvr214, c215-16, 217, c218, 219, c220,
221, 223, 226; c301, 304, 308-9, c310-14,
317, f318, 319, 321, c323, 324-26, c327,
328; c401, c402, c405, c407-9, 410, c411,
413, c415, 416, c417-19, 420-22, 424,
c425, 426, 428, 430-33, c434, c437.
    see /si/ c15, c35, c44, c50; c105, c109,
cvr113; c220, c225; c311, c320, c322,
c*324; c405, c429.
    seed /sid/ cvr308; c423.
    seen /sin/ c5-8, c13, c15, c19, 20, c22,
cvr25, c27, c35, c39, †40, c41, c46, c48,
50, c51, c56-57, c59, c64; c101, c105,
c107-9, cvr112, c113-14, 115, 122, cvr130,
cvr133, c135, c138-39, 142-43, 145, 149;
c203-4, cvr209, c212, cvr220, c224,
cvr225; 301, c302-3, 305, *306, cvr308,
cvr314, c315-16, c320, cvr322, c323;
cvr403-4, c405, c407, c409, c414, cvr416,
c417, c423, c427-28, cvr429, c435.
    no response 36; 118, 151; 222; 307; 406,
412, 436.

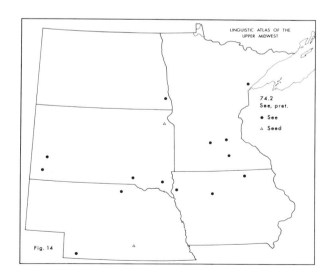

Fig. 14

Comment:
saw: Used as participle—22, 27; 115,
132; 301. seen: "'Seen' isn't proper"—55.

shrink

21.8 The apron shrank. NE 660. VF 20-21.

As in the eastern states, shrunk strongly dominates the UM as the preterit of
shrink, in all five states and among the
three speaker types. Although current dictionaries generally list shrank before
shrunk, the implication that it is the
majority form is belied by the evidence
that, on the contrary, shrank is distinctly a minority variant.

No pronounced social or regional contrast appears, but Type II speakers do
evince slightly less preference for
shrank than do those of Type I.

A solitary instance of shrinked in the
speech of a Nebraska Type I inf. of New
York State parentage reflects the infrequent appearance of that variant in New
York and eastern Pennsylvania. Four infs.
(28, 46, 116, 142) exhibit some ambivalence, either voluntarily replacing their
originally proffered shrunk by shrank or
expressing doubt about the proper form.
One southern Iowa inf. mildly disparaged
the form not his own by remarking of
shrank, "That's Yankee talk."

The South Midland regional variant with
the initial cluster /sr/ is recorded by
five different fws. in the speech of 12
infs., eight of whom are in Midland speech
territory. Five of these have South Midland parentage. The /sr/ speakers are 13,
16; 125, 130, 132, 137-38; 204, 223; 314;
409, 414.

Shrenk, recorded by fw. M in Duluth, is
almost certainly a mere phonetic variant
of shrank.

	Type I	Type II	Type III
shrank	20%	12%	20%
shrunk	83%	90%	80%

	Mn.	Ia.	N.D.	S.D.	Nb.	Ave.
shrank	14%	17%	8%	18%	25%	12%
shrunk	92%	86%	92%	82%	75%	86%

shrank /ʃræŋk, sræŋk/ 5, cr28, cr35,
*43, 45, *46, 52; 101, 114, :?116, 118-19,
126, 131, 139, cr142; 209, 223; 309-10,
318-19, 324; 416, 423, 425-29, 433-34.
shrenk /ʃrɛŋk/ 16.
shrinked /ʃrɪŋkt/ 413.
shrunk /ʃrʌŋk, srʌŋk/ 36-38, 41-43, 46-
47, 49-51, 53-54, c55, 59-61; 102-13, 115,
:?116, c117, 120-25, 127-30, 132, :133,
134-39, 140-41, ?142, 143-52; 201-8, 210-
22, 224-26; 301-5, *306, 307-8, 311-15,
*316, 317, 320-23, 325-28; 401-11, 414-15,
417-22, 424, c426, 430-32, 435-37.
no response 6, 19, 32, 39-40, 44, 48,
56-58, 62-65; 412.

sit

39.4 Sit down. NE 318. VF 21.
39.5 I sat down. NE 661. VF 21; F18.

Although the *Oxford English Dictionary*
states that in "modern use" sit and the
related causative verb set are "clearly
distinguished," an early confusion between them certainly persists in the
United States. In the Atlantic states,
the North Central region, and the UM both
items requiring a form of the verb sit
yield a good number of responses with the
form set. This confusion is compounded by
those who use sit as a preterit and the
few who have sit as both present and past.

In a situation calling for an invitation
to be seated at the dinner table about 70%
of the UM infs. offer the imperative,
i.e., sit down or set down, or, occasionally, a phrase, as let's sit down, here
included as a valid instance of the base
form of the verb. (For the other lexical
responses see Volume 1.) Of these infs.
83% use sit, and 17%, rather scattered,
use set. Of the latter, two-thirds are
Type II's. No college speakers have set in
this context.

Sat, the historical preterit of sit,
predominates in all five states, with set
providing, however, 26% of the total. The
geographical distribution is fairly even,
except for a lower incidence of set in Nebraska, but the social contrast is conspicuous. As with the imperative, most of
the set responses come from Type I speak-

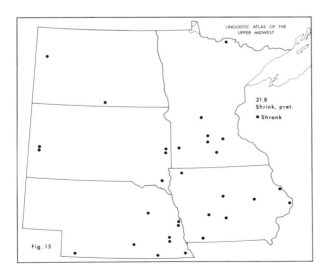

LINGUISTIC ATLAS OF THE
UPPER MIDWEST

21.8
Shrink, pret.
● Shrank

Fig. 15

ers (36). Fifteen are in Type II, and one Minnesota user of set is in Type III.

Three-fourths of the infs. offering sit as the imperative or base form also consistently have sat as the preterit. One-fourth, mostly in Type I, have the sit-set pair; two Type I's, in Minnesota and Iowa, have sit-sit.

Slightly more than one-half of the UM infs. with set as the imperative also have it as preterit, as in the Middle Atlantic states. A smaller number have the set-sat combination. One Type I Minnesotan has set as imperative and sit as past. A Type I Iowan of South Midland background has the set-sot combination reported by Atwood as not uncommon in the South Atlantic states, as does one Minnesotan of Quebec and Michigan parentage.

Imperative:

sit /sɪt/ 1-2, 4, 7-11, c14, 17-18, 20-23, 25, 28-29, 32-34, 36-38, 41-42, 45, 48-50, s54, 56-57; 102, 104-8, 110, 112-14, 117-23, 126-32, 134, 136-43, 145-46, 148-49; c201, 202-3, 207-9, 212-13, 221-23; 301, 306, 310, 312-13, 315, 318, 321, 324-26; 401-4, 406, 408, 411, 417-18, 422, 430, 432, 436-37.

set /sɛt/ 13, c15, 17, 31, 35, c51, !52, 64; 109, 115, 124, 133, 135, 147; 205, 225; 305, 314, !320, c327; 425, 429.

other response 3, 5-6, 12, 16, 19, 24, 26-27, 30, 39-40, 43-44, 46-47, 53, 55, 58-63, 65; 101, 103, 111, 116, 125, 144, 150-52; 204, 206, 210-11, 214-20, 224, 226; 302-4, 307-9, 311, 316-17, 319, 322-23, 328; 405, 407, 409-10, 412-16, 419-21, 423-24, 426-28, 431, 433-35.

Preterit:

	Type I	Type II	Type III
sat	60%	88%	93%
set	37%	15%	7%
sit	8%	1%	0
sot	3%	0	0

	Mn.	Ia.	N.D.	S.D.	Nb.	Ave.
sat	75%	63%	83%	76%	77%	74%
set	23%	33%	29%	24%	19%	26%
sit	3%	4%	8%	4%	7%	5%
sot	3%	2%	0	0	0	0

sat /sæt/ 2-5, 7, 9-13, cvr14, 16-17, 19-20, 22-23, 25-26, cvr!28, 29-30, 32-34, 36-45, 47, 49-50, 53, cvr54, 55, 57-61, 63-65; 101-4, 106, 108, 110-12, 118-21, 123-24, 126-29, c130, 131, 134, 136-38, 141, 145, 148-49; 201, 203, 207-11, c212, 213-23, 226; 301, 304-8, 310, 313, c314, 315-19, 321, 323-26; 402, 409-13, c414, 416-18, 420-21, c422, 424-28, cvr430, 431-33, 435-36.

set /sɛt/ 1, 6, 8, 13, c15, 18, 21, 24, c35, c42, 46, c51, !52, 56, 62; c102, 105, 107, c109, 114, c115-16, 117, 135, 139-

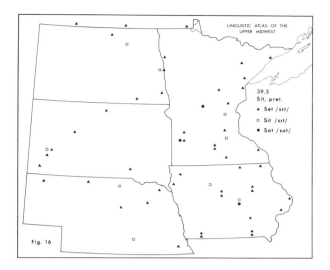

Fig. 16

40, 142, c143, 146-47; c201, 202, 205, 207, cvr220, 224-25; 302-3, 311, c312, c320, 322; c401, 403, c407, c414, 415, 434.

sit /sɪt/ 31, 48; 113, cvr132; c212, cvr220; 311; 405, 423.

sot /sɑt/ 27, c46; 133.

other response 122, 125, 144, 150-52; 204, 206; 309, 327-28; 404, 406, 408, 419, 429, 437.

spoil

37.6a The meat is spoiled. NE 206. VF 21.

Although a few synonymous responses occur (see Volume 1), most of the 185 infs. who reply to this item (155 or 91%) offer either of two forms of the verb spoil as the participial adjective in the context given above or similar ones. Of the 155 infs. who do use spoil 84% have spoiled and 18% have spoilt, each with the /ɔɪ/ diphthong. There are no examples of the recessive eastern variant with /aɪ/.

Both social and regional variations appear in the data. In the eastern and North Central states spoilt is most frequent in Midland speech territory. Consistently, in the UM it is most frequent in Iowa. Again, in the eastern and North Central states spoilt is more likely to be used by old-fashioned and less-educated speakers. Consistently, in the UM one-fourth of the Type I infs. have spoilt but only one-tenth of the Type II's have it. It barely survives among educated speakers with two instances in South Dakota and Nebraska, Midland territory. Over all,

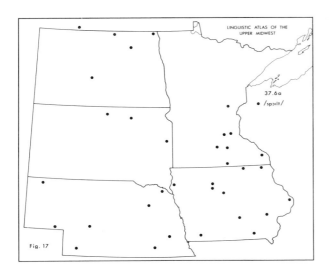

tered incidence includes in the South Midland territory of Iowa only three infs. of
South Midland parentage.

A social range is apparent, however, in
the contrast between the 13% frequency of
sweated among Type I infs. and the bare 5%
frequency among Type II's. One Minnesotan
and one North Dakotan contribute the only
Type III occurrences.

	Type I	Type II	Type III
sweat	86%	94%	81%
sweated	14%	5%	13%

	Mn.	Ia.	N.D.	S.D.	Nb.	Ave.
sweat	87%	96%	88%	93%	92%	89%
sweated	5%	10%	12%	4%	9%	10%

   sweat /swɛt/ 1-2, ¹3, 4, c5, 6-10, 12-
14, c15, 16-19, 21, f22, 23-34, 36-37,
cr39, 40-41, !42, 43-45, !46, ¹47, 49-53,
55, 57-65; 101-15, 117, 119-30, ?131, 132-
34, 136, 138-43 145-46, 148-50; 201-5
207, 210-21, 223-26; 302-21, c322, 323,
!¹324, 325-28; 401-5, !407, 408-19, 421,
423-29, 431, 433-37.
   sweated /swɛt+d/ 11, c13, 35, 38, ?39,
47, sn48, 54, 56; 116, 118, 135, 137, 144;
206, 209, 222; 301; 420, 422, 432.
   no response 3, 20; 147, 151-52; 208;
406, 430.

spoilt is probably a declining form that
is giving way to regular _spoiled._

The following percentages refer only to
the number of infs. responding with a form
of _spoil._

	Type I	Type II	Type III
spoiled	76%	92%	85%
spoilt	26%	10%	15%

	Mn.	Ia.	N.D.	S.D.	Nb.	Ave.
spoiled	94%	72%	79%	89%	78%	84%
spoilt	11%	31%	21%	11%	22%	18%

   spoiled /spɔild/ 1-12, c13, 14-15, 17-
23, c25, 26-28, s30, :31, 32-36, 39-46,
c47, 48-50, c51, 52-56, 58-60, c61, 62,
64-65; 101-2, 104, 106-8, 110, 115-16,
118-21, 123, s124, 128-29, 131, 136, 140-
41, 144-45, 147-49; 202-3, 205, :sn206,
208-10, c211, 213-15, 217-18, c219, 222-
26; 301-2, 304-5, 307-8, :!309, 310, 312-
16, 318-26, c327, 328; 402-4, c405, 406,
408-13, 416-17, 419-25, 427-28, 430-31,
433-35, 437.
   spoilt /spɔilt/ 24, 35, 38, c49, c51,
57, 63; 105, c107, 109, 112-14, 134, 138-
39, 142, 146; 201, 204, 207, 212, c216;
303, 306, sn317; :401, 407, 415, 418, 426,
429, 432, 436.
   other or no response 16, 29, 37; 103,
111, 117, 122, 125-27, 130, 132-33, 135,
137, 143, 150-52; 220-21; 311; 414.

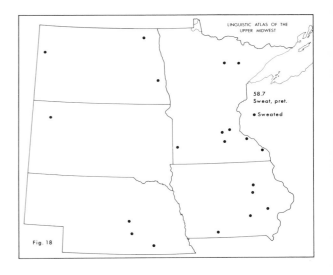

swim

69.4 I _swim_ across. NE 579. VF 23.

As in the eastern states, _swam_ strongly
predominates throughout the UM as the
preterit of _swim._ The popularity of the
variant _swum_ in the Middle and South Atlantic states is only weakly reflected in
its greater frequency in Iowa and Nebraska

sweat

58.7 He _sweat_ hard. NE 662. VF 22.

As in New England and all the North Central states but Kentucky, the preterit of
sweat is simple _sweat._ The South Midland
preference for _sweated_ does not clearly
persist in the UM, where its widely scat-

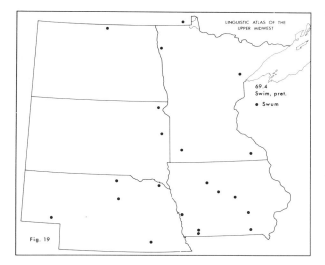

LINGUISTIC ATLAS OF THE
UPPER MIDWEST

69.4
Swim, pret.
• Swum

Fig. 19

than elsewhere in the UM. This decrease,
together with the fact that all examples
are from the speech of old-fashioned
infs., attests its continuing obsolescence.

	Type I	Type II	Type III
swam	85%	97%	100%
swum	18%	5%	0

	Mn.	Ia.	N.D.	S.D.	Nb.	Ave.
swam	95%	86%	96%	93%	92%	91%
swum	9%	16%	4%	7%	14%	11%

swam /swæm/ 2-6, c8, 9, cr10, 11-14, 16-
58, c59, 60-63, *64, 65; 101-12, 114, 116-
17, 119-24, 126-31, 133-34, 136-41, 143-
45, 147-50; 201-3, cr?204, 205-13, c214,
215-26; 301-6, 308-16, 318-28; 401-5,
408-12, 414-16, 418-31, 433-37.

swum /swʌm/ 1, 7, ?10, 15, 40, !¹47, 59,
†62, 64; 113, 115, 125, 132, 135, 142,
c143, 146; 204; 307, 317, ¹327; 405, 407,
413, 417, 432.

no response 118, 151-52.

Comment:
swam: "That would be proper"—204.
"Sounds like a funny word. Swum is just
as funny"—327. swum: "A boy might say
this"—47. Used by inf. as a child—62.

take

58.5a He took his medicine.
58.5b Haven't you taken your medicine?
NE 664. VF 23; F19, F30.

For the preterit and past participle of
take the varied forms reported by Atwood
have been reduced to three in the UM.
Took is well-nigh universal as the preterit; taken is universal as the participle.

Two minor eastern preterit variants
survive in the UM. Southern and South
Midland taken is the form used by six
Type I infs.: one Canadian, one Minnesotan with an Oklahoma father, one North
Dakotan of German parentage and another
with Illinois parents, and a Nebraskan
whose father probably was born in Kentucky. Tuck, dominantly Southern but with
a few scattered examples in the north-
east Atlantic region, occurs only three
times in the UM, likewise in the speech
of Type I infs.: one Canadian, a North
Dakotan with Norwegian parents, and a
South Dakotan whose father came from
Maryland.

The single participial variant is took,
which, though widely scattered in the
eastern states, is used by only two UM
infs., a Type I Minnesotan and a Type II
Nebraskan.

These findings are supplemented by the
data for the lexical items 58.1 and 58.2
(see Volume 1), both of which often elicit
a form of take. For 58.1 all such infs.
use took except inf. 429, who uses taken
consistently here as elsewhere. For 58.2
all use took except the North Dakotan,
214, who during the interview first re-
plied with taken but then switched to
"correct" took.

Preterit:
taken /tekən/ cvr3, c35; 214; 305, 316;
cvr429.
took /tʊk/ c3, 5, 7, cvr14, cvr15,
cvr16, 17, sn19, 24-26, 28, c29, 30, c31,
35-38, cvr41, 45-46, 49, 54, 57, 60-62;
101-50; c201, 202-8, cvr209, 210-14, c215,
216-19, c220, 221-24, cvr225, 226; 301,
c302, 303-4, 306-11, c312, 313-15, 317-19,
321-26, c327, 328; c401-2, 403-6, c407,
408, c409, 410-11, c412, cvr413, 414,
c415-16, 417, c418-19, 420-21, c422, 423-
25, c426-28, cvr430, c431, 432-35, c436,
437.
tuck /tʌk/ c201, cvr216; c320.
other or no response 1-2, 4, 6, 8-13,
18, 20-23, 27, 32-34, 39-40, 42-44, 47-48,
50-53, 55-56, 58-59, 63-65; 151-52.

Past Participle:
taken /tekən/ 1-12, c13-14, 15-20, c21-
22, 23-35, c36, 37-40, cvr41, 42-43, c44,
45-65; 101-41, c142, 143-50; 201-24,
cvr225, 226; 301-28; 401-13, c414-15,
416-17, c418-19, 420-25, cvr426, 427-29,
431, 433-37.
took /tʊk/ c57; 432.
no response 151-52; 430.

teach

73.2 Who taught you that? NE 666. VF 24.

Unlike the eastern states, the UM typically has only a small minority (14%) of users of <u>learn</u> in the indicated context. The 86% who use a form of <u>teach</u> are unanimous in choosing <u>taught</u>. No examples of <u>teached</u> occur. See <u>learn</u> above, and for the specific infs. using <u>taught</u>, see Volume 1.

tear

74.3a The road was all <u>torn</u> up. NE 665. VF 64.

Standard <u>torn</u> predominates among all speakers and in all states of the UM. The variant <u>tore</u>, heavily favored by less-educated infs. in northeastern New England and in Pennsylvania, Ohio, and Kentucky, is likewise more common with Type I speakers in the UM, particularly in Iowa and South Dakota. But even there it is not the majority form, and its weak showing in the more recently settled portions of Nebraska and Minnesota indicates that it is now recessive.

	Type I	Type II	Type III
tore	42%	26%	7%
torn	60%	75%	93%

	Mn.	Ia.	N.D.	S.D.	Nb.	Ave.
tore	27%	40%	28%	42%	25%	32%
torn	75%	64%	72%	58%	75%	70%

tore /tor/ sn4, 7, c16, 24-25, 30-31, 34, 41, sn48, 52, 54, 56-57, !¹58, 60, 63-64; 104-8, c109, 112-13, 115, 117, c*124, 125, 135, 138, 140, 143, 146-49; 207-9, 212, 215-16, 224; 301, ¹302, 303, 305-8, 311, 316, 322-23, 325; 401, 405, 407-8, s414, 417, 421, 424-25, 427.

torn /torn/ 1-3, 5-6, 8-15, 17-19, *20, 21-23, 26-29, 32-33, 37-40, :*41, 42-47, 49-50, c51, c53, 55, 58-59, 61-62, 65; 101-3, 110-11, 114, 116, 119-24, 126-34, 136-37, 139, 141-42, 144-45, 149-50, 152; 201-3, 205-6, 210-11, 213-14, 217-19, :220, 221-23, c225, 226; 302, 304, 309-10, 312-13, c314, 315, 318, 320-21, 324, 326-28; 402-4, 406, 409-16, 418-20, 422-23, 426, 428, 430-31, sn432, 433-37.

no response 35-36; 118, 151; 204; 317, 319; 429.

Comment:
  tore: "We say that a lot"—4. Inf. says this is the usual form here—58.

throw

25.4 He <u>threw</u> a stone at the dog. NE 667. VF 24.

The distribution of the preterit of

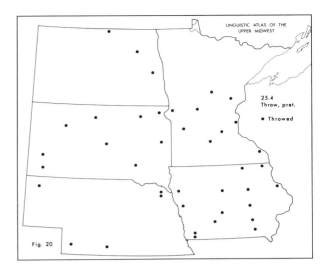

LINGUISTIC ATLAS OF THE UPPER MIDWEST

25.4
Throw, pret.

• Throwed

Fig. 20

throw is remarkably like that of <u>tear</u>. Standard <u>threw</u> dominates all types in the UM. The variant <u>throwed</u>, common among less-educated speakers in northeastern New England and in the Midland areas of Pennsylvania, Illinois, and Ohio, is likewise strongest with Type I speakers in the UM, noticeably in the older areas as well as in western South Dakota. Its higher frequency in Iowa and in South Dakota reflects its Midland orientation, and its low frequency in Nebraska suggests that it is becoming recessive.

Although as a child in North Dakota fw. A heard other boys use the variant <u>thrun</u>, it did not appear during fieldwork.

School emphasis upon the standard form has led to uncertainty among some infs. One Type III inf. uses both <u>threw</u> and <u>throwed</u>, as do three Type II's and eight Type I's. Inf. 21 has <u>threw</u> both as preterit and as participle.

	Type I	Type II	Type III
threw	77%	94%	100%
throwed	31%	9%	6%

	Mn.	Ia.	N.D.	S.D.	Nb.	Ave.
threw	92%	82%	87%	75%	89%	86%
throwed	15%	27%	13%	32%	14%	19%

threw /θru/ 1-14, c15-16, 17-18, c19, 20-23, 25-26, 28-34, c36, 37-38, c39, 40, 42-55, 57-65; 101-4, 106, 108, 110-18, 120-28, 130-31, 133-34, 136-41, 144-50, 152; 201-3, 205-10, !211, 213-19, 221-26; 301-2, 304-5, 308-10, 312-13, 315-16, 318-21, 323-28; 401-6, 409-20, cvr422, 423, 425-26, c427, 428, 431-37.

throwed /θrod/ c21, 24-25, 27, 35, c40, 41, c51, c56; 105, 107, c109, c114, 117, c119, 122, c127, 132, 135, 142-43, 146, 151; c204, 212, c220; c302-3, 306, c307,

cvr311, c314, c317, 320, c322; c401, 407-8, cvr429, c430.
no response 129; 421, 424.

Comment:
throwed: Used as participle—c42; 225; 404, c407, cvr418, cvr422, c429.

wake

70.6 I woke up early. NE 668. VF 25; F20.

The regularizing trend increasingly evident as English-speaking settlers moved west from the eastern states did not eliminate all the minor variations resulting from the intricately involved history of four different but related verbs. For them see awake, awaken, and wake in the *Oxford English Dictionary*.
In the indicated context the common eastern and North Central woke, as the preterit of wake, is likewise the form offered by three-fourths of all UM infs., with a preponderance among Type I speakers, less among Type II's, and only a bare majority among Type III's.
Approximately four out of five of all UM infs. using woke add the completive up. The proportion is higher (89%) in the three western states than in Minnesota and Iowa (69%).
Unlike woke, the form awoke exhibits some measure of social and regional variation. It is used by about one-eighth of all UM speakers, but they are unevenly distributed. It is favored by Type II infs. more than by the less educated, and it is much less frequent in the Dakotas.
Wakened, a still more uncommon variant, is somewhat more frequent in Minnesota, North Dakota, and Canada than elsewhere, and it is typically a Type III form. The related awakened, not found at all among Type I infs., is likewise more likely to appear in educated speech. It is scattered in four UM states but not found in North Dakota.
Waked (up), described by Atwood and Virginia McDavid as an older Southern and South Midland variant, consistently is used by Type I speakers in Iowa and Nebraska but once also in Minnesota.
As a preterit, wake is a rare UM variant. One Minneapolis Black has it, and it slipped into the conversation of a St. Paul inf. of French-Canadian parentage. It occurs once in Nebraska. All three infs. are in Type I.
Five infs. offer a participial form in a passive phrase, not specifically sought by the fw. Was awakened is the response of 44, 47, and 53; was woke up is used by

53 and 404, the latter in free conversation.

	Type I	Type II	Type III
awakened	0	7%	13%
awoke	6%	20%	19%
wake	3%	0	0
waked	5%	1%	0
wakened	6%	6%	25%
woke	84%	73%	56%

	Mn.	Ia.	N.D.	S.D.	Nb.	Ave.
awakened	6%	4%	0	4%	3%	4%
awoke	14%	16%	8%	4%	19%	13%
wake	3%	0	0	0	3%	2%
wakened	11%	2%	12%	4%	8%	7%
woke	75%	78%	81%	89%	67%	77%

awakened /əwekənd/ 14, 34, 57, 61; 131, 136; 304; 406.
awoke /əwok/ 12, 18, 22, 28, 30, 40, 50, 60, 63; 101, 103, 108, 112, 120, 126, ?130, 137, 145; 203, ?214, 225; 319; 402, 404, 412, 428, 431, 436-37.
wake /wek/ 35. wake up c36; 434.
waked up /wekt/ 33; 124, 132-33; 401, 403.
wakened /wekənd/ 1-2, 20, 25, 40, 42, 46; 122; 201, ?211, cr214, 222; 319; 414, 418, 426.
woke /wok/ ?26, 27, 31, 35, 45-48, 58, c59, 60-62; 117, 121, 127, 129, 131, 133-35, 140, 144, 146-49; 208; 313-14, 325; 413, 416, 423-24, 433-35. woke up 3-11, c13, 14-17, 19, 21, 23-24, ¹25, cr26, ¹28, 29, 32-33, 37-39, 41, 43-44, 49, 51-56, 64-65; 102, 104-11, 113-16, 119, s120, 123, 125, 128, 136, 138-39, 141-43, 150; 202, 204-7, 209-10, cr211, 212-13, 215-21, 223-24, 226; 301-3, 305-9, 311-12, 315-18, 320-24, 326-28; 402, 405, 407-11, 415, 417, 419-22, 425, 427, 429-30, 432.
no response 118, 151-52.

Comment:
woke up: "You hear the old Irish people say this"—25.

wear

57.7 He is worn out. NE 480. VF 25.

The standard past participle worn dominates the replies of the three inf. types throughout the UM.
The variant wore, which is given by nearly one-third of the Type I speakers in southern New England, eastern New York, and northern New Jersey, persists in the same proportion in the UM. Both in the East and in the Northern speech sector of the North Central states wore is much less frequent among the high school graduates than among Type I speakers; the same is true in the UM. The Midland ori-

31

entation of wore, evidenced by its high frequency in Maryland, West Virginia, Indiana, and Kentucky, is not reflected in the UM, however, unless the slightly higher incidence in Nebraska can be so interpreted.

The usual context for this item is as indicated above, but sometimes the reference is to a thing instead of a person, as "I've worn out several cars"—1; "Have you worn another one [pencil] out?"—11; "When our clothing was wore out . . ."—203; "I haven't wore one [garment]"—429.

	Type I	Type II	Type III
wore	36%	13%	13%
worn	68%	88%	93%

wore /wor/ or /wɔr/ 9, c19, 21, 25-26, 31, 34-36, sn48, 51, s56, c60, 63, *64; c104, 109, 112-13, 129, c133, 140, 143, 146, 149; c203, 207, 209, 216, 220, 224; 302-3, 311, c322, 323; 401, 403, c405, 407, 417, 422-23, 427, c429, cvr430, 436.

worn /worn/ or /wɔrn/ c1, 2-8, 10, c11, 12, 16, 19-20, 22-24, 27-28, cvr29, 30, 32-34, 37-44, c45, 46-47, 49-50, cvr51, 52-55, 57-58, c59, 60-62, 65; 101-8, 110-11, 114-28, 130-32, 134-39, 142, 144-45, c147, 148, 150; 201-2, 204-6, 208, 210-15, 217-19, 221-23, 225-26; 301, 304, 309-10, 312-15, 318-22, 324-28; 402, 404, 406, 408-13, 415-16, 418, c419, 420-21, f422, 424-26, 428, 431, sn433-34, 435, 437.

no response 13-15, 17-18; 141, 151-52; 305-8, 316-17; 414, 432.

write

72.7 I have written to him. NE 670. VF 26.

Apparently only one of the nonstandard variants of the past participle of write survived the western migration. Standard written is strongly favored by all three inf. types in the UM. Correspondingly, wrote, which predominates among Type I speakers in the East and still has a one-third frequency among the less educated in the North Central states, is used by only one-fifth of the Type I infs. in the UM and by fewer than one in 10 of the high school graduates. No Type III inf. has it. In light of this circumstance and the fact that most of the examples of wrote are in the older portions of the UM, wrote is clearly a declining form.

Uncommon eastern writ, wroten, and write are not reported at all.

	Type I	Type II	Type III
written	79%	92%	100%
wrote	22%	9%	0

Fig. 21

72.7
Write, ppl.
● Wrote

	Mn.	Ia.	N.D.	S.D.	Nb.	Ave.
written	81%	85%	96%	93%	84%	86%
wrote	21%	15%	4%	11%	16%	15%

written 1-4, 6, 8-15, 17-28, 32-34, 37-39, c40, 41-44, 46-47, 49-51, 53-55, 57-60, 62-63, 65; 102-4, 106-11, 113-14, 116, 119, c120, 121-33, 136-39, 141-45, 148-50, 152; 201-19, 221-26; 301-10, c312, 313-20, 322-27; 401-6, 408-14, 417, c419, 420-26, 428-31, 433-37.

wrote 5, 7, 16, :30, 31, 35, :36, 45, 48, 52-53, 56, 64; 105, 112, 115, 135, 140, 146-47; 220; c311, c314, 321; 407, 415-16, c418, 427, 432.

no response 29, 61; 101, 117-18, 134, 151; 328.

Comment:
written: Inf. uses writ as the preterit—302; c422.

PRESENT INDICATIVE PERSONAL FORMS

be

21.6 Be as a finite verb. NE 677. VF 27; F21.

As a finite form, be, not found at all in the Middle and South Atlantic states but occurring as a relic in New England, New York, Wisconsin, and Michigan, has only a ghostly existence in the UM.

Actually only two bona fide instances appear in the field records, both from the free conversation of Type I speakers in Minnesota and northern Iowa. Seven other infs. have the form as heard or no longer used.

The specific examples are given below.

"They be coming home about midnight": in past context—cvr4. "How be you?": inf. thinks it humorous—23; inf. calls it southern—[1]39; inf.'s aunt used it—s[1]40; inf. considers it Irish—[†]48; heard occasionally from old people—[1]65. "I be going"—[1][†]25, s[†]48. "Be I on the right road?": inf. frequently uses <u>be</u> in this way—c105.

be (am I? are they?)

20.7a-b <u>Am I (Are they)</u> going to get some? NE 675. VF 35.

Because of the difficulty of eliciting a response in this or a similar context and because the responses obtained were uniform, fws. bypassed this item in nearly one-half of the interviews.

Although both <u>be</u> and <u>is</u> are reported by Atwood as occurring in Type I speech in the East and the South, the only UM deviation from standard <u>am</u> and <u>are</u> is that of Minnesota Type I inf. 44, who asks "Is they?" in conversation. There are no examples of the omission of the finite verb.

Both <u>am</u> and <u>are</u> occur with the whole range of pronunciation from fully stressed [æm] and [ɑr] to weakly stressed [m̩] and [ɚ], the variation depending entirely upon semantic stress and not upon regional or social factors.

do

10.8 He <u>does</u>. NE 687. VF 27; F22.

The third person singular of <u>do</u> is recorded in any context where it occurs under stress with the personal pronoun. Standard <u>does</u> /dʌz/ is well-nigh universal in the UM. South Atlantic <u>do</u> unaccountably appears in Minnesota, although there but once in conversation. Rare New England <u>dooz</u> /duz/ barely survives in the speech of two older residents of Hutchinson, Minnesota. The general uniformity of responses sometimes led fws. to omit this item.

do /du/ [1]2, c8, s[1]23, [1]34, [†]40, sn41, [1]42, s[†]48.
does /dʌz/ 10, 13-14, c16-17, 18, 23, 29-31, 33-34, 39-40, 44-45, f46, c47, s48, 49, 52-63, 65; 101-6, 108-16, c117, 119-27, 129-30, 132-34, c135, 136-46, f147, 148-50, 152; 210, 214, c217, 218, 221, 223; c301, 302-4, 306, 308, 312,

316-20, 323, c325, 326, 328; 401-2, 404-6, 408, 411-16, c417, 418, 420-37. /d+z/ c415. /duz/ c44-45.
  no response 1, 3-7, 9, 11-12, 19-22, 24-28, 32, 35-38, 43, 50-51, 64; 107, 118, 128, 131, 151; 201-9, 211-13, 215-16, 219-20, 222, 224-26; 305, 307, 309-11, 313-15, 321-22, 324, 327; 403, 407, 409-10, 419.

Comment:
  do: "Old country people use this"—2. Used by inf.'s aunt from New England—40. Heard but condemned—42. Very rare—48.

have

10.6 I've heard about it.
11.2a-b <u>I've</u> been thinking. NE 682, 683. VF 26; F12.

Unstressed <u>have</u> occurs with the personal pronoun <u>I</u>, or sometimes <u>we</u> or <u>they</u>, and a following past participle in the indicated perfect phrase contexts.

Before <u>heard</u>, <u>I have</u> occurs without exception as /aɪ-əv/ or /aɪv/. Before <u>been</u> this contraction is also the usual form for one-half of the Type I speakers, three-fourths of the Type II speakers, and four-fifths of the college group.

But, both in the East and in the UM, before <u>been</u> a phonetic process produces a significant result in the speech of one-half of the less-educated infs., one-fourth of the Type II's, and, rarely, even a college graduate or two. In this position before <u>been</u> the weakly stressed /v/ of <u>have</u> becomes only /ʋ/. This sound assimilates easily with the /b/ to become

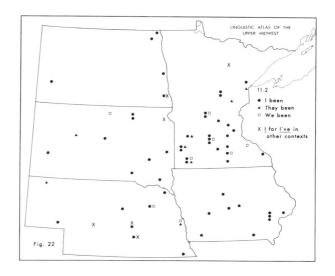

Fig. 22

a rather weak bilabial continuant [β]. In rapid or casual speech such assimilation may then become total, so that the overt effect is the omission of have and hence the apparent use of been as a finite verb, as in I been thinking.

	Type I	Type II	Type III
I been	50%	25%	17%
I've been	60%	78%	83%

	Mn.	Ia.	N.D.	S.D.	Nb.	Ave.
I been	47%	19%	63%	56%	32%	38%
I've been	71%	78%	50%	50%	68%	69%

I been /ai bɪn/ c15, c21-22, 27, cvr28, c29, c32, c35, 37, c42-44, 45, c46-48, cvr50, c51, c56, c59, cvr60, c62; 114, 126, 128, 132, 137-38, cvr140, 142, 146, 152; c206-7, c214, c220, c225; cvr305, 306, c311, 314, 319, c322, c324, c327; cvr407, c414-15, c417, c421, cvr422, c436. they been /ðe bɪn/ 17, c23, c42, c46, c60; c302; c401, c428. we been /wi bɪn/ 27, c44, cvr50, c55, c59; c303; c415, c427.

I've been /aiv bɪn/ 4-6, 10, c13, 14, 18-20, 26, cvr28, cvr30, c31, c33, c35, 36, c38-39, 40-41, c44, c46-47, 49-50, c53, 54, c55, c57-63, c65; 101-4, s105-6, 107-8, 110-13, 115-17, 119-25, 127-30, s131, 133-36, 139, 141, c142, 143-45, 147-50; c201, 214, 218, 221; 301, 304, 306, c309-10, 320-21, c325, 326; c402, cvr403, 404, c405, 406, 408, c410, 411, c416, 418, cvr422, s424, 427, c429, 432, 437. I have been /ai hæv bɪn/ 423, s425, 431, 433, 435. they've been /ðev bɪn/ c405. we've been /wiv bɪn/ 412, 428.

no response 1-3, 7-9, 11-12, 16, 24-25, 34, 52, 64; 109, 118, 151; 202-5, 208-13, 215-17, 219, 222-24, 226; 307-8, 312-13, 315-18, 323, 328; 409, 413, 419-20, 426, 430.

Third Person Singular

The third person singular, present indicative, was not sought specifically but was incidentally recorded in replies to 15.2 "She rinses the dishes," 50.7 "He resembles his father," and 68.4 "It costs too much."

All examples are of the standard -s ending, phonetically varied according to the nature of the final sound of the verb base. For special variations with costs see Volume 3.

There are no instances of the zero ending (the absence of -s), reported by Atwood as an infrequent South Atlantic form, and more recently identified as one of the characteristics of so-called Black English.

NUMBER AND CONCORD

were

21.4a-b-c We/You/They were. NE 679. VF 28-29.

Were follows a plural subject with greater frequency in the UM than in the eastern and North Central states. Two-thirds of all infs. use were in all three persons. Only in the third person does competing was, thanks to the ambivalent use of both forms by some speakers, attain as much as 49% frequency. The contrast between the two forms is primarily social, but a possible regional difference appears also.

In the first person were or was occurs typically with we as subject. Unlike New England and the Middle Atlantic states, where was is well-nigh universal with Type I speakers, the UM presents a situation in which not much more than one-half of the Type I's use was, and none of the college graduates. The regional distribution indicated in the table below is puzzling, since it does not accord with the typical Northern/Midland contrast or with the contrast often appearing between Minnesota and Iowa, on the one hand, and the Dakotas and Nebraska on the other, with respect to old-fashioned or nonstandard forms. The irregularity may be due to a difference among fws., with respect to their noting conversational forms.

	Type I	Type II	Type III
was	60%	30%	0
were	53%	76%	100%

	Mn.	Ia.	N.D.	S.D.	Nb.	Ave.
was	30%	49%	53%	47%	44%	42%
were	80%	51%	60%	63%	69%	66%

we was c4, c19, cvr16, cvr20, c21, c24, cvr25, c26, 27, c31, c35, c42, c48, c51, c59; c105, c107-8, cvr113, c115, c117, c121, 125, c132, c135-36, c138-40, c142-43, c145, 146, c147-48, 149; c203-4, cvr207, c209, cvr216, c218, c220, c225; c301-2, 303, 307, cvr311, c314, c323, c*324; c401, c403, c405, cvr407, cvr413, c414, cvr416, c417, c424, 425, c427, c429, c432, c436.

me and my wife was c35. my brother and me was c301. he and I was c311. him and I was c311. another fellow and I was c320.

we were 1, c3-4, 5-6, c7, 8, c10, c13-14, 17, cvr20, c21-23, 24, 31-32, c33, 34, 38-41, c43, c47, 48-50, c51, 53-55, c58, c60-63, 64-65; c101-2, 103-4, c106, 110-11, 113-14, 120, 122-24, 126-28, c130, 133, c134, 137, 141, f150, 152; c203, 205, c208, c211, 214, c216-17, c221, c224; 304, cvr305, 309, 312, c313, 321, c323, 324, c325, 326-28; 402, 406, 410-12, c414, 415-16, c417, c419, 420-23, s424, 426-28, 430, cvr431, 433, 435, c437.

him and my older sister were c31.

no response 2, 9, 11-12, 15, 18, 28-30, 36-37, 44-46, 52, 56-57; 109, 112, 116, 118-19, 129, 131, 144, 151; 201-2, 206, 210, 212-13, 215, 219, 222-23, 226; 306, 308, 310, 315-19, 322; 404, 408-9, 418, 434.

In the second person were or was occurs with you as subject. Despite the modern use of you as both singular and plural, the tendency to use was is no greater than with we, and its distribution among the types and in the UM as a whole is similar to that of the third person.

	Type I	Type II	Type III
was	63%	25%	0
were	48%	80%	100%

	Mn.	Ia.	N.D.	S.D.	Nb.	Ave.
was	27%	48%	86%	31%	52%	42%
were	80%	55%	14%	93%	52%	64%

you was 6, c16, c21, c31-32, ¹39, c43, c46, c48, c51, c59, c60; c107-8, c114, c116, 117, c119, *124, 127, c135, c140, c142-43, 145, c148, 149; c203, c209, c212, c215-16, c218; 303, c311, c314, c317, c*324; 401, c402-3, c405, c409, c414, 415, c*417, c418, c422-23, c425, c429, 432, c434, c436.

you were 1, c3, 5, 19-20, 24, 26-27, 33-34, 36, 38-41, 45, c46-47, 49-50, c51-52, 53-55, 58, c59-63, 64-65; 102, 105, 110, 113, 120, 122-24, 126, 128, 130, c131, 134, 139, 141, 146, f150; 214; 302-4, 309, c311, 312, c313, 321, 323-24, 326, 328; 406, 410-11, 413, 416, 420-21, 423, 427-28, 430-31, 433, 435, 437.

no response 2, 4, 7-15, 17-18, 22-23, 25, 28-30, 35, 37, 42, 44, 56-57; 101, 103-4, 106, 109, 111-12, 115, 118, 121, 125, 129, 132-33, 136-38, 144, 147, 151-52; 201-2, 204-8, 210-11, 213, 217, 219-26; 301, 305-8, 310, 315-20, 322, 325, 327; 404, 407-8, 412, 419, 424-26.

In the third person were or was occurs usually with they as subject, although conversational examples with plural nouns as subjects appear in the records as well. Those with was are listed below. The distribution in the third person plural approximates that with we and you except that two of the Type III infs. have was.

	Type I	Type II	Type III
was	65%	30%	18%
were	58%	79%	82%

	Mn.	Ia.	N.D.	S.D.	Nb.	Ave.
was	35%	54%	69%	53%	56%	49%
were	86%	46%	46%	60%	74%	67%

they was c16, 19, 21, c23, c35, ¹39, c44, c46, c48, c50, c52, c59, c*60; c107-9, c115-17, c121-22, 124, 127, cvr132, c133, c139-40, 143, c145, c147, 148-49; c207, c212, c215-16, c218, c220; c301, c303, c311, c314, cvr320, cvr322, c*324; cvr401, c403, 404, c405, c414, cvr415, c416, c417-18, c422, cvr429-30.

them eyes was, their feet was, his father and mother was c31. the logs was cvr41. the first fences was c52. him and another fellow was c56. some of the old ladies that was c203. the grass roots was, the Republicans was cvr216. the railroad irons was c220. things was c224; cvr429. the REA boys was c301. those doors was c303. these soldiers was c314. the stock cars was cvr320. the rocks was, my older brothers was cvr322. my son and his wife was c325. those cats was c401. these was c405. my feet wasn't cvr407. my folks was, those trees was c417. some teachers was cvr418. our pastures wasn't c418. them was 429. our turkeys was c432.

they were c1, c3, 5-6, c8-10, 13, c15, 19, c20, 21, c23, 24-27, c29-30, c32, 33-34, 38-41, c44-45, 46, c47, 49, c51-52, 53-55, c56, 57-58, c59-63, 64-65; c101, 102, 104-5, 110, 113, 120, 122-23, 126, 128, 130, c131, 134, 141, c146, f150; 201, c209, 211, 214, c215, c220; c301, 302, 304, 309, 313, 321, 324, 326, 328; c402, c404, 406, 410-11, c412, 413, 415, c417-19, 420-21, c422, 423, cvr428, c429, 430-31, 437.

no response 2, 7, 11-12, 14, 17-18, 22, 28, 36-37, 42-43; 103, 106, 111-12, 114, 118-19, 125, 129, 135-38, 142, 144, 151-52; 202, 205-6, 208, 210, 213, 217, 219, 221-23, 225-26; 305-8, 310, 312, 315-19, 323, 327; 408-9, 424-27, 433-36.

here are

21.1 Here/There are your clothes. NE 357, 678. VF 29.

For many people Here's and There's seem to have become unit formulas not affected by the demand for grammatical agreement with a following plural noun (clothes or other plural). This tendency, very strong among Type I and Type II speakers in the eastern United States and the North Central region, persists in the UM, where it yields a four-fifths dominance of is over are among Type I infs. and a three-fifths dominance among Type II's. But all Type III speakers use the competing standard English are.

The summary below does not distinguish Here and There examples. The difference in their frequency is not significant, as it is almost certainly due to the nature of the dramatic situation set up for this item by the fw., a situation in which a parent calls a child's attention to the nearby location of clothing for which the child is searching at a distance.

Twelve infs. are recorded as using both is and are, a practice quite likely much more common than the data indicate.

	Type I	Type II	Type III
Here are	24%	49%	100%
Here's	81%	59%	0

	Mn.	Ia.	N.D.	S.D.	Nb.	Ave.
Here are	42%	33%	60%	33%	41%	40%
Here's	63%	67%	55%	71%	70%	66%

here are /hɪr ɑr/ ¹2, 3, 7, 9, 14, 17-18, 20, 26, 28, 34, 36, 38, 47, 49-50, 53-55, 58, 63, 65; 101, 103, 106, 110-11, 114, 119-20, 126, 133, 137, sn139, 150, sn152; 201, 205, 211, 214-19, 222-23, 226; 309-10, 312-13, 318-19, 326, 328; 401-2, 406, 410-11, 413, 418-21, 426, 428, 433, 435. there are /ðɛr ɑr/ c1, cvr26, cvr30, cvr53, c61; 415, 420, 428.

here's /hɪrz/ c5, c13, 19, 23-24, 27, 32, :35, 39-41, !44, 46, 51, c56-57, 59, 62; 102, 104-5, 107-9, 112-13, 115, 121, sn124, sn129, 132, 134-35, 138, 140-46, 149; 203, 220; 301-3, sn304, 305-8, 311, *316, :321, 322-24; 404, 407, 409, 414-17, 422-25, 427, 429-32, 434, 436-37. here is /hɪr ɪz/ 10, 31; 117, 127. there's /ðɛrz/ c6-7, c21, cvr24, cvr26, c29, cvr30, c32, c36, 37, 42, c43, c48, c57, c60; 116, 128; cvr401, c403, 405, c408-10, c412, 416, cvr417, 421, c422, 423-24, 427, 430-32, c436. there is /ðɛr ɪz/ c4, 10, c25, c51, c56, c62, c64-65; c201, c204-5, 212; c323; c401, cvr414.

no or other response 11-16, 22, 33, 45, 52; 118, 122-23, 125, 130-31, 136, 147-48, 151; 202, 206-7, 221; 315, 317, 320, 328.

ashes are

7.6b Ashes are white. NE 331.

Although the grammatical number of both oats and ashes may be considered ambiguous, ashes, much more than oats, is treated as plural. As in New England, the infs. of all types throughout the UM prefer ashes are. Is occurs in the speech of one-fifth of the Type I speakers and one-tenth of the Type II's. It is not a Type III usage.

A possible slight Northern orientation of ashes is can be inferred from its

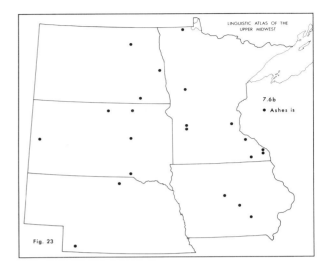

greater frequency in Minnesota and the Dakotas than in Iowa and Nebraska, but the difficulty in obtaining this response and the high number of "no responses" make this inference rather shaky.

are 1-3, 5, 7-8, 10-12, 20-24, 26-28, 31-34, 36, 38-40, 43-52, 54, 58-63; 102-14, 116-17, 123-24, 127-30, 132, 134, 137, 139-43, 145-49; 201, 203-6, 208-11, 213-19, 221-23, 226; 301-2, 304, 311, 313-15, 321-22, 324-27; 401-4, 406-11, c413-14, s415, 416-25, f426, 427-28, 430-31, 433, s434, c435, 436-37.

is 4, 19, c37, †40, 41-42, 55-57, 64; 115, 133, 135; 212, 220, 224; 303, 305, 309, *316, 323; 405, †409, 429.

no or forced response 6, 9, 13-18, 25, 29-30, 35, 53, 65; 101, 118-22, 125-26, 131, 136, 138, 144, 150-52; 202, 207, 225; 306-8, 310, 312, 317-20, 328; 412, f426, 432.

oats are

34.5 Oats are thrashed. NE 128. VF 30.

The distribution of competing oats are and oats is in the UM does not reflect that in the eastern states, where are is stronger in New England and New York State and is dominates in the Middle Atlantic states. Atwood, indeed, writes: "Except in the Midland it appears that the singular verb is receding rapidly."

In the UM, on the contrary, the singular concord with is appears to have won acceptance in historically Northern speech areas, Minnesota and North Dakota, and even among Type III speakers. As a result, the over-all relative frequency in the UM is about fifty-fifty.

36

Several fws. record other instances of singular concord with <u>oats</u>: <u>averages,</u> 212; <u>grows,</u> 9, 209; <u>requires, 324;</u> <u>rip</u>-<u>ens,</u> 37, 220. These are not tabulated below.

are 1-3, 12, 14, 16, 20, 23, sn27, 28-30, 32-34, 38-40, 43-45, c46, 47-49, c51, 52-54, 58-61, 63; 101-6, 109, 111, 113, 116-23, 125-29, :130, 131, 133, 137, 140, 143-49, 152; 201-2, 217, 226; 309-10, 315-16, 320, 328; 404, 406, 410-11, c413, c416, 420, 423, 426-28, 431-33, sn434, 435, 437.

is 4-6, c7, 8, 10, 13, 15, 17-19, 21-22, 24-26, 36, ¹40, 41-42, 50, c51, 55, sn56, 57-58, 61, f62, 64, sn65; 107-8, 112, 114-15, 124, 132, 134-36, 138-39, 141-42, 150; 203-8, 210-11, 213, 215-16, 218-19, 221, 223-25; 301-5, sn306, 312, c313, 314, 318, 321-23, 325-26; 401-3, 407, 409, 412, 414, c415, 417, c418, 421, c422, 424-25, 429, c430, c*432, 436.

no or other response 9, 11, 31, 35, 37; 110, 151; 209, 212, 214, 220, 222; 307-8, 311, 317, 319, 324, 327; 405, 408, 419.

Comment:
are: Inf. offers both: "Depends on how you speak"—58. Inf. says either but thinks <u>are</u> is "correct"—61. <u>is</u>: Inf. says this is a "Down Eastern" way of speaking—40.

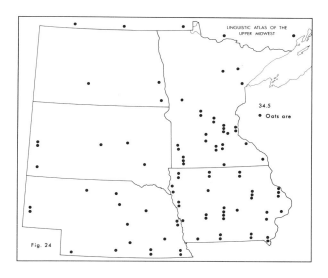

NEGATIVE FORMS

am not

The first-person present-tense negative is recorded in two contrasting contexts,

one declarative and the other interrogative.

21.2a I <u>am</u> <u>not</u> going to hurt him. NE 673. VF 3̲0̲.

The negative declarative appears in the indicated or a similar context. Two expressions are offered by the infs.: <u>I'm</u> <u>not</u> and <u>I</u> <u>ain't</u>. In New England the majority form is <u>I'm</u> <u>not</u>, but <u>ain't</u> and <u>hain't</u> are common among less-educated speakers. In the Midland states <u>ain't</u> is the majority form among Type I speakers; in the North Central region it also dominates in that group and it is used by two-fifths of the Type II's. Atwood reports its use by six cultured speakers in New England and two in the Middle Atlantic states.

With UM infs. <u>ain't</u> is less popular than in the East, although it retains its Midland orientation. It is the usual form for less than one-half of the least educated group, only a fourth of the Type II speakers, and none of the college graduates. No instances of <u>hain't</u> occur.

<u>I'm</u> <u>not</u> is the majority form for all groups in all the UM states but South Dakota; it is strongest in Minnesota and North Dakota.

	Type I	Type II	Type III
I ain't	46%	26%	0
I'm not	58%	83%	100%

	Mn.	Ia.	N.D.	S.D.	Nb.	Ave.
I ain't	29%	34%	30%	57%	28%	34%
I'm not	80%	66%	70%	52%	83%	71%

I'm not /aɪm nɑt/ 1-7, 10, 13, 17-21, 23-24, 26, 28, c32, 33-34, c38, c40, *41, c42, c44-47, 49-50, c52-53, 54-55, c58, 60-61, c62-63, 65; 101, c102, 103-4, 106, c108, 110-15, c116-17, c119-20, 121-23, 125-26, ?128, 131, 133, 136-37, 139, ?145, 149, f150, 152; c204, 207, 214, c216, 217-18, 221; 304, 309-10, 312-13, 318, 321, 324, c325, 326, 328; 401-4, 406, 408, 410-16, c417, 420-21, 423, s424, 425, 427-28, 431, 433, 435, 437.

I ain't /aɪ ent/ c16, ¹18, c19, c26, 27, c31, c39, 41, c42, c44, 48, c51, c54, c57, c59, 64; c105, c107, c109, 121, 124, sn127, 130, 132, *134, 135, c138, c142, 143, c146-47; 207, c220, c224; c301, 302-3, 306, c311, c314, 316-17, 320-21, c322, c*324; c404, 405, 408, 418, 421, c427, c429, 430.

no response 8-9, 11-12, 14-15, 22, 29-30, 35-37, 43, 56; 118, 129, 140-41, 144, 148, 151; 201-3, 205-6, 208-13, 215, 219, 222-23, 225-26; 305, 307-8, 315, 319, 323, 327; 407, 409, 419, 422, 426, 432, 434, 436.

21.3 <u>Am</u> <u>I</u> <u>not</u>? NE 676. VF 30-31.

The negative interrogative occurs typically as a tag question but sometimes in other contexts.

Three expressions are widespread: <u>ain't</u> <u>I</u>, <u>am</u> <u>I</u> <u>not</u>, and <u>aren't</u> <u>I</u>.

Historical <u>am</u> <u>not</u> <u>I</u>, which in England became <u>amn't</u> <u>I</u> or <u>a'n't</u> <u>I</u>, earlier /ænt aɪ/ and then /ɑnt aɪ/, appears only in the single Canadian example /ɑnt aɪ/ provided by an Ontario inf. both of whose parents were born in Great Britain.

<u>Ain't</u> in <u>ain't</u> <u>I</u> represents the normal phonetic development of earlier /ænt/ with a lengthened vowel, i.e., /æ:/. (Compare, for example, the Shakespearean pronunciation /næ:m/ and /tæ:k/ for <u>name</u> and <u>take</u> with Modern English /nem/ and /tek/.) But, quite likely because school grammarians objected to the analogical extension of <u>ain't</u> to the second- and third-person constructions as a replacement for <u>aren't</u> and <u>isn't</u>, the form itself became objectionable. As a dog with a bad name, <u>ain't</u> was hence condemned even in its solidly based use in the inverted negative interrogative, so that most educated speakers avoid it.

Both in the eastern and in the North Central states <u>ain't</u> <u>I</u> is actually the most common expression; in the UM it is used by just one-half of all recorded infs. Two-thirds of the oldest and least educated speakers have it and almost one-third of the high school graduates. One university graduate, a Minnesota farmer and stockbreeder, uses it regularly except in the presence of his wife, who insists upon his saying <u>aren't</u> <u>I</u>. One Iowa farmer has <u>hain't</u> <u>I</u>.

<u>Am</u> <u>I</u> <u>not</u>, an alternative historical contruction, is often preferred as "correct" by Type III speakers despite its aura of formality. In the Northern speech territory of the UM two-thirds of the responding college graduates report their use of <u>Am</u> <u>I</u> <u>not</u>, as do nearly one-half of the high school graduates and nearly one-third of the least educated group. It has a rather clear Northern orientation, being most frequent in Minnesota and North Dakota. Several infs. indicate that in a formal situation they switch to this from their customary <u>ain't</u>.

To avoid the undesirable social implications of <u>ain't</u> <u>I</u> and the uneasy stiffness of <u>Am</u> <u>I</u> <u>not</u>, some speakers resort to the bizarre and illogical <u>aren't</u> <u>I</u>. Whether a spelling pronunciation of the British spelling "aren't I" for present-day British /ɑnt aɪ/ or /ɑnt aɪ/ or an analogical extension from <u>aren't</u> <u>you</u>, this form appears to be either gaining slightly in acceptance or more acceptable in the UM. At the time of the New England survey more than 40 years ago only 23 infs. offered it, about 5%. Virginia McDavid reports only four examples in the North Central states. But there are 19 occurrences in the UM, and it is proportionately more frequent among the two younger groups and less so among the oldest and least educated.

	Type I	Type II	Type III
ain't I	63%	45%	9%
am I not	29%	45%	64%
aren't I	5%	15%	27%

	Mn.	Ia.	N.D.	S.D.	Nb.	Ave.
ain't I	41%	47%	52%	62%	58%	50%
am I not	53%	20%	52%	35%	30%	39%
aren't I	9%	20%	4%	9%	8%	11%

ain't I /ent/ sn6, 7, sn11, 12, 19, c23, c25, 26, 30, c36, c39, 41, c44, !†45, 47-48, 50, c51, c57, 64; 105, 107-9, 117, 121, 124, 127, 130, 132, 134-35, sn140, 142-43, 146-47, †150; 203-4, 206-7, 209, ¹210-11, ?213, !¹214, 215, c216, 217-18, 220, 223, 225, †226; 301-2, c303, 308-9, c311, ¹313, 315, !321, 323, c*324, 325, 328; 401, !¹403, 404-5, 407-8, :409, †411, 412-13, 415, c416, 418-19, ¹420, 421-22, !423, 425, 429-30, 432, 436, sn437. hain't I /hent/ 115.

am I not 1-2, 4-5, 7-8, 10, 20-22, 24, 28-29, 32, 37-38, 40, *41, 45-46, ¹47, 49, 53-54, 58, 60-63, 65; 104, 106, 111, 113, 116, 120, 123, 131, f150; 201, 205, 208-14, !217, 219, 226; 304, 312-13, ?314, 318-19, ?320, 324, 326-27; 402-3, 406, !411, 414, 417, 426, f427, 431, 433, f434, 435, 437.

a'n't I /ɑnt/ 3.

aren't I 9, c26, 33, 37, 50; 101, s?114, 122, 125-26, 128, ?133, 136, 139, ?145, 149; 202; 308, 310, ?320; 401, 410, 428, s433.

no response 14, 16-18, 27, 31, 34-35, 42, 55; 102-3, 110, 112, 118-19, 129, 137, 141, 144, 148, 151-52; ?221, 222, :?224; 305-7, 316, 322; 424.

Comment:

ain't I: Inf. would use this occasionally, but he is aware of its social status—7. Formerly used by inf.—45; 226; 411. "We wouldn't say 'am I not' but 'ain't I'"—47. Usu. avoided in his wife's presence—50. "But 'am I not' is proper"—207. Usu.—209, 217; 437. Inf. dislikes this expression—211; 313. "'Ain't' isn't the correct word, but that's what I'd probably say"—308. "'Am I not' is pretty nice"—309. Inf. uses this when "in a hurry"; her husband always says it—401. Usu. avoided—419. "Can I use 'ain't I?'"—423. "Everybody says this"—436. <u>am</u> <u>I</u>

not: Inf. says 'ain't' was drilled out of
h‾i‾m‾ in school—8. Inf. has prejudice
against 'ain't'—10. "I always said that"—
212. Usu. avoided by inf.—226; 304. Inf.
says it is an unnatural form—312. n‾o‾ r‾e‾-
s‾p‾o‾n‾s‾e‾: "I don't use 'ain't' too o‾f‾t‾e‾n‾.
M‾i‾g‾h‾t‾ say, 'That's right, isn't it?'"—34.
Inf. avoids this type of tag question—55;
103, 110; 222.

are not

21.2c They a‾r‾e‾ n‾o‾t‾ going to hurt him.
NE 674.

The third-person present plural negative of b‾e‾ appears in the indicated or a
similar c‾o‾n‾t‾e‾x‾t‾. Four expressions occur:
T‾h‾e‾y‾ a‾i‾n‾'‾t‾, t‾h‾e‾y‾ a‾r‾e‾ n‾o‾t‾, t‾h‾e‾y‾'‾r‾e‾ n‾o‾t‾,
and t‾h‾e‾y‾ a‾r‾e‾n‾'‾t‾. T‾h‾e‾ l‾a‾s‾t‾ three are tabulated t‾o‾g‾e‾t‾h‾e‾r‾ as instances of a‾r‾e‾.
The incidence of a‾i‾n‾'‾t‾ here is l‾o‾w‾e‾r‾
than with the first- a‾n‾d‾ third-person
singular constructions, but its frequency
is consistently higher among the less-
educated infs. One Minnesota farmer, a
Type III inf., uses it freely. One instance of South Midland h‾a‾i‾n‾'‾t‾ is included from the speech of a T‾y‾p‾e‾ I‾ Iowan of
Kentucky and Tennessee parentage.
The variations with a‾r‾e‾ dominate in all
states of the UM and a‾m‾o‾n‾g‾ all three
groups.

	Type I	Type II	Type III
ain't	38%	17%	10%
are not, etc.	66%	83%	90%

	Mn.	Ia.	N.D.	S.D.	Nb.	Ave.
ain't	24%	27%	40%	40%	17%	26%
are not, etc.	80%	70%	80%	60%	87%	75%

they ain't /ðe ent/ c15, c19, c27, c43,
50, c51-52, c56-57, c59; c105, c107, 121,
c124, sn127, *134, 142-43, 147; 207,
c220, c225; 302-3, 311, c314, 317, 320,
c322; c401, 405, 430, 432, c436. they
hain't /ðe hent/ c135.
they are not /ðe ɑr nɑt/ 21, 49; ?145.
they're not /ðɛr nɑt/ 1-5, 10, 20, 23-24,
28, 32-34, c40, 41, c52, 54-55, 58, c59,
64-65; c102, 103, 109-10, 112-14, c117,
120-21, 133, 137-40; 207, 214, 221; 304,
309, c321, 324, 326, 328; 402-3, 408,
413-14, 416, 420-21, 423-24, 427, 431,
437.
they aren't /ðe ɑrnt/ 7, 14, 26, c43,
c47, c53, c61-63; c102, 106, 111, 122-23,
126, ?128, 130-31, 136, 146, 149, f150;
218; 310, 312-13; 401, 406, 410-12, 422.
no response 8-9, 11-13, 16-18, 22, 25,
29-31, 35-39, 42, 44-46, 48, 60; 101,
104, 108, 115-16, 118-19, 125, 129, 132,

141, 144, 148, 151-52; 201-5, 208-13,
215-17, 219-20, 222-23, 224, 226; 301,
305-8, 315-19, 323, 325, 327; 404, 407,
409, 415, 417-19, 425-26, 428-29, 433-35.
Comment:
a‾i‾n‾'‾t‾: Inf.'s wife gets after him if he
uses 'ain't'—122. "I try not to say it
because it don't sound good"—127. Inf.
has carefully taught himself to avoid
'ain't'—312. "I try not to say 'ain't,'
but do sometimes without thinking"—424.

didn't use to

55.6 She d‾i‾d‾n‾'‾t‾ u‾s‾e‾ t‾o‾ be afraid. NE
700. VF 33‾.‾

The negative of u‾s‾e‾d‾ t‾o‾ is usually recorded in the c‾o‾n‾t‾e‾x‾t‾ a‾b‾o‾v‾e‾.
As in the East and the North Central
states, d‾i‾d‾n‾'‾t‾ u‾s‾e‾ t‾o‾ is the dominant
form in t‾h‾e‾ U‾M‾ among all infs.
One minor variant, u‾s‾e‾n‾'‾t‾ t‾o‾, is
sparsely spread with s‾i‾x‾ i‾n‾s‾t‾a‾n‾c‾e‾s‾ among
Type I and II speakers in the Northern
speech area (one in Canada), although Atwood reports all but three of the eastern
examples as found in Maryland and northern Virginia. A rare eastern variant,
u‾s‾e‾d‾ n‾o‾t‾ t‾o‾, is offered by two older
i‾n‾f‾s‾.‾ i‾n‾ M‾i‾n‾n‾e‾s‾o‾t‾a‾ and Nebraska.
More than 10% of the UM infs., like
some in New England and New York, apparently are frustrated by the problem of
negating u‾s‾e‾d‾ t‾o‾ and resort to n‾e‾v‾e‾r‾ as a
negative m‾a‾r‾k‾e‾r‾. Only one Type I‾I‾I‾ speaker, however, has this solution.

	Type I	Type II	Type III
didn't use to	82%	78%	85%
never used to	6%	18%	8%
used not to	2%	0	0
usen't to	4%	4%	0

	Mn.	Ia.	N.D.	S.D.	Nb.	Ave.
didn't use to	70%	94%	71%	88%	80%	80%
never used to	17%	4%	13%	8%	17%	12%
used not to	2%	0	0	0	3%	1%
usen't to	4%	2%	13%	0	0	3%

didn't use to /dɪdənt jus tə/ 1-3, sn6,
7-9, sn10, 12-14, 16, 20-23, c25, 26,
:sf?27, sn29, 30, 32, f35, c36, 37-40,
42, f43-44, f46, s47, sn48, 49-51, 54-57,
61, ¹62, 63, 65; 101-19, 122-26, 128,
sn129, 130-31, sn132, 133-39, 141-43,
145, sn146, 147-48, 150; 201, 203-5,
sn207, 208, 210-11, 214, :f216, 217-19,
221-23, c225, 226; 301, c302, 303-4, 308-
10, c311, :fn312, 313-14, sn315, 316,

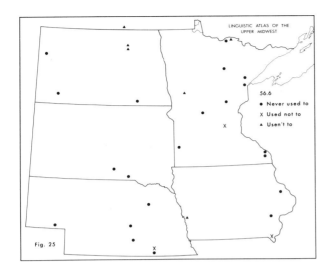

Fig. 25

sn318, ¹319, sn320, sn322, 324-28; c401,
:402, 403-4, c405, 406-8, ?409, 410-12,
414-16, c417, 418, sn419, 420, 425, c428,
429, 431, s433, sn435, sn437.
   never used to 5, 12, c15, 17, 24, 28,
47, 57-58; 121, 152; 209, 215, 224; 321,
323; c415, 421, 423, 433, 436.
   used not to 33; 149; sn432. used to not
!¹42.
   usen't to /jusənt tə/ 5, 19, :?36,
s¹58; 125; c202, 212, :!213.
   no response 11, 18, 31, 34, ?41, 45,
52-53, 59-60, 64; 120, 127, 140, 144,
151; ?206, ?220; 305-7, 317; 413, 422,
424, 426-27, 430, 434.

Comment:
   didn't use to: "That's the way it would
be here"—6. Inf. considers this improper—
62. Inf. avoids this; says it sounds unnatural—319. usen't to: Inf. says this
shows a lack of education—58. Used by
inf.'s uncle (born in Ireland)—125.
"'Usen't' isn't a word"—225.

does not

11.1 He doesn't care. NE 688. VF 28.

   In the UM don't and doesn't occur as
the contracted forms of the third-person
singular negative of do. The item was
usually sought in the context indicated
above, but it was often recorded in other
contexts as well, such as "That don't
hardly sound right"—44; "Grandma don't
want that in the house"—203; "A little
politeness don't hurt people"—10; and "It
doesn't show"—47.
   Type I and Type II speakers in the UM

retain the typical eastern and North Central preference for don't. Despite school
injunctions it is still favored also by
nearly one-half of the Type III speakers,
some of whom shift from don't to "standard" doesn't in accord with the social
situation. In the suggested context 10
infs. (five I's, four II's, and one III)
offer school-taught doesn't but in free
conversation use don't. Ten others (six
I's, three II's, and one III) are recorded as using both don't and doesn't in
free conversation.

	Type I	Type II	Type III
doesn't	26%	51%	77%
don't	88%	60%	46%

	Mn.	Ia.	N.D.	S.D.	Nb.	Ave.
doesn't	45%	42%	33%	14%	41%	40%
don't	72%	67%	80%	91%	70%	74%

   doesn't /dʌzənt/ c3, 4, c7, c13, 14,
c17, 18, 20, c23, 24, 26, 28, c32, 37,
40-41, c44, c47, 49, c52, 53-54, c58, 60,
c61-62, 63; 102-4, 106, 108, 110-11, 113-
14, 116, c122, 126, 129, c130, 131, c134,
137-38, 150, 152; 201, c203, 214, 221,
223; 304, cr324, 326; 406, 411, c413,
414, 416, 421, 423, 425-27, c428, 430-31,
s432, 433-35.
   don't /dont/ c1, c3, 4, c5, 6, c7, 8,
c10-11, c15-16, c19, c21-25, c27, c29-32,
c34-36, c38, 39, c42-48, c50-51, c55-57,
c59, c62-63, c65; 101, 105, c107, 109,
112, c113, 115, c116-17, 119-20, c121-22,
123-25, c127-29, 132-33, c135, 136, c137,
c139, cvr140, c141-43, 145-49; c203-4,
c207-8, c211, c216-18, c220-21, c224,
cvr225; c301, 302-3, 306-8, c309, c311,
c314-15, 316, c317, 318, c320-22, ?324,
*324, c325, c327; c401, 402, c403-5,
c407-9, c411, 412, c414-18, c420, 422,
c424, cvr427, c428-30, c432, c434, 436-
37.
   no response 2, 9, 12, 33, 64; 118, 144,
151; 202, 205-6, 209-10, 212-13, 215,
219, 222, 226; 305, 310, 312-13, 319,
323, 328; 410, 419.

Comment:
   don't: Usu.—4. Inf. laughs over his
"incorrect grammar" but says he always
uses 'he don't'—120.

have not

10.7 I haven't done it. NE 684. VF 31.

   The first-person present negative of
have is usually recorded in the context
given above. Although 10 infs. respond
with the full have not, most use one of
four contracted expressions: I've not, I
haven't, I ain't, and I hain't.

Considered as a class, I've not and I haven't together dominate the three inf. types in the UM. They account for all the Type III responses, nearly all of the Type II, and three-fourths of those in the least educated group.

Ain't and hain't in this construction are only superficially like the ain't and hain't contractions of the verb be. Actually they are not the same. They represent a normal phonetic development of an unstressed have not, i.e., from [hævn̩t] to [hæᵛnt] to [hæːnt] to [hent] and [ent]. But guilt by association has so blackened the reputation of this ain't that it, too, is generally considered to be mildly disreputable. It remains viable only in the speech of slightly more than one-third of the less-educated infs. And as with the other ain't, some infs. vary between the standard and the nonstandard expressions.

	Type I	Type II	Type III
haven't/ 've not	72%	97%	100%
ain't/ hain't	38%	9%	0

	Mn.	Ia.	N.D.	S.D.	Nb.	Ave.
haven't/ 've not	87%	84%	73%	82%	86%	84%
ain't/ hain't	22%	22%	36%	32%	14%	23%

ain't /ent/ c7, c13, c15, c25, c27, c31, c35, c51, c54, c56-57; c105, 117, 124, 130, 135, c139, c142, 146, c147; c204, c209, c212, c220, c224; 301, c302, c311, c317, c322, c*324; c405, c407, c418, c422. hain't /hent/ 118, 135; c303.

have not /hæv nɑt/ 5, 28, 33, 42, 50; 104; 214; 317; 434-35. I've not /ɑɪv nɑt/ c410.

haven't /hævənt/ c2, f4, 7-8, 10, c14, 16, c17, 18, c19, 22-24, 26, 28, c29, c31, 32-33, :34, 38-39, c40, 41-43, c44-47, 48-49, c51-53, 54-55, c57-63, 64; 101-2, 105-12, 114, 116-17, 120, 122-23, 125-27, c128, 129, 132-34, 136-38, c139, 140, c141, 143-45, c146, f148, 149-50, 152; 207, 210, 214, 217-18, c220, 221, 223; 302, 304-6, 308-10, 312, 314, 317, 319-20, 323, c324, 325-26, c327, 328; c401, 402-3, 406, 408, 411-15, c416, 421, 425, c426, 427-28, c429, 430-33, c434, 435, 437.

no response 1, 3, 6, 9, 11-12, 20-21, 30, 36-37, 65; 103, 113, 115, 119, 121, 131, 151; 201-6, 208, 211, 213, 215-16, 219, 222, 224, 226; 307, 313, 315-16, 318, 321; 404, 409, 417, 419-20, 423-24, 436.

21.2b He/She is not going to hurt him. NE 674.

The third-person present negative appears in the indicated or a similar context.

Ain't is about as common in the third person as in the first. Nearly one-half of the Type I speakers and nearly one-third of the Type II's use it. One college graduate alternates it with isn't. No instances of hain't appear.

He's not and he isn't, combined, generally account for two-thirds of the recorded responses. In about one-fourth of the interviews, especially in North Dakota, the fw. did not seek or obtain a third-person response at all.

	Type I	Type II	Type III
ain't/ is not/ isn't	48%	30%	10%
	52%	75%	100%

	Mn.	Ia.	N.D.	S.D.	Nb.	Ave.
ain't/ is not/ isn't	39%	24%	67%	45%	39%	37%
	65%	75%	45%	55%	68%	66%

he ain't c6, 11, 19, c22, c25-27, c31, c35, c42-46, c48, c51, c57, c59, c62; cvr105, c115, 121, 124, sn127, *134, c139, c142, 143, 147; c204, c206, 207, c209, c212, c220, c225; c301, 302-3, cvr311, c316-17, c322-23, 320; 404, 407, c409, 411, 415, c417, 418, c423, c429, c430, c432, 434.

he isn't 3, 7, 10, c18, c23, 24, 26, 28, c32, c40, 50, c52-53, 54-55, c61-63, 64-65; 102, 104, 106, 109, 111, c116, 117, c120, 122-23, 126, ?128, 130-31, c136, 138, ?145, 146, 149, f150; 207, 214, 218, 221; 304, 309-10, 312-13, 321, c325, 326, 328; 401, 403, 406, 408, 410-12, 414, 420, 422-24, 431, 437.

he's not 1-2, 4-5, 20-21, 23, 33-34, 36, 41, 49, 58; 101, 103, 107, 110, 112-14, 120-21, c125, 133, 137-39; 324; 402, 413, 416, 421, 427.

no response 8-9, 12-17, 29-30, 37-39, 47, 56, 59-60; 118-19, 129, 132, 135, 140-41, 144, 148, 151-52; 201-3, 205, 208, 210-11, 213, 215-17, 219, 222-24, 226; 301, 305-8, 314-15, 317-19, 327; 405, 409, 419, 425-26, 428, 433, 435-36.

45.5 He ought not to. NE 698. VF 32-33.

Despite prescriptions in some handbooks and some dictionaries, no one negative expression with ought has uniform acceptance as being standard. Some infs. even insist that ought has no negative form.

According to Atwood, the eastern Midland and South Midland areas typically have the contraction oughtn't and the Northern area has hadn't ought along with ought not and oughtn't in southern New England. Although Virginia McDavid finds ought not most common in the North Central states, she reports also that one-fourth of the Northern area infs. have hadn't ought and one-fourth of the Midland area infs., mainly those in Kentucky, have oughtn't to. All forms are found in each of the three inf. groups.

The UM reflects the complexity of the eastern situation. The three ought constructions occur in each of the three groups of infs. but with uneven distribution. Nearly one-half use the full ought not, but only one-tenth the contracted oughtn't. One-fifth have hadn't ought. At least one-fourth can express the negative only by resorting to shouldn't. One Minnesota inf. solves the problem by putting the negative marker in the following infinitive phrase, e.g., "She ought to not play," and an Iowan by using never before ought.

Ought not itself occurs fairly uniformly throughout the UM, with greatest frequency in Minnesota and least in Iowa. The Midland orientation of oughtn't does not appear in the UM, where, although Iowa exhibits its use, its lowest frequency is found in the strong Midland speech state of Nebraska. One interpretation of this circumstance is that it is consistent with other data showing decrease in less common grammatical forms in the three western states of the UM.

Hadn't ought, presumably Northern in orientation, turns up occasionally in southern Iowa. It is consistently more common in North Dakota than in Nebraska.

Although of the various expressions none can be considered exclusively standard, ought not is offered by most of the college graduates and by nearly one-half of the middle group. But each of the other forms is also represented in the speech of Type II and Type III infs.

A curious result of the rejection of any ought forms by one-fourth of the recorded infs. is that they thereby lack an easy device for expressing a contrast between the stronger ethical obligation some infs. feel when they use ought and the weaker situational desirability these infs. feel when they use should. Several ought-less infs., queried about how they would make this distinction, admitted their inability to do so.

	Type I	Type II	Type III
hadn't ought	26%	19%	13%
ought not	43%	46%	53%
oughtn't	13%	9%	13%
shouldn't	19%	35%	20%

	Mn.	Ia.	N.D.	S.D.	Nb.	Ave.
hadn't ought	16%	34%	25%	21%	15%	22%
ought not	61%	36%	55%	43%	41%	45%
oughtn't	13%	15%	14%	10%	3%	11%
shouldn't	16%	21%	14%	38%	49%	26%

hadn't ought :8, 10, 19, ¹34, 40, ¹42, fs45, 57-58, 60, 64; 105, s106, 109, 113-14, 118, s121, 122-23, f125, s?128, 132, 135, 138-42, c147; 203-4, 211-12, sn217, 218; 303, c311, c314, 325; 401, 405, 407, 412, 429.

never ought 116.

ought not 1-4, 7, 9, 11-12, 20-23, 28, 30-32, 34, 36-37, 39, 41-42, f43, 44, f46-47, 49-50, 55, 61-63, 65; 101-2, 104, 110-12, 116, 119-20, 126, 128-31, :136, 143, f144-45, 146, f148; 202, 205, 208, 210, 213, 215, :216, 217, 219-20, 225; 304, 306, 309, 313, ¹315, 320, 324, 326-28; 402-4, 406, 408-9, 411, 413-14, 417, f418, 419, 422, s?425, 426, 431, s435, *436, 437.

oughtn't 6, 24-26, 33, 35, 54, 56; 108, 115, 117, 133, 137, 149-50; 201, :f209, 221; 301, 316; s432.

ought to not 48.

shouldn't 6, c13, 14-18, 25-30; 121-22, 125, 127-28, 130, 134, 144-45, 148; 207, 216, 226; 305, 307, 313, 316, 318-19, 321, 323; 402, 410, 415-16, 418, 420-21, c423, 434-35, 427-28, 430, 433-37.

no response 5, 26-29, 51-53, 59; 103,

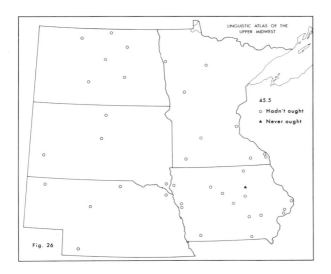

LINGUISTIC ATLAS OF THE UPPER MIDWEST

45.5
○ Hadn't ought
▲ Never ought

Fig. 26

107, 124, 151-52; 214, 222-24; 302, 308, 310, 312, 317, 322.

Comment:

hadn't ought: Inf. says 'oughtn't to' "goes against the eardrums"—10. shouldn't: "'Oughtn't' doesn't sound like a word"—321. no response: Inf. insists there is no negative for 'ought'—5.

was not

21.5 It wasn't me. NE 604. VF 32; F24, F30.

In this or a similar context the negative of the preterit singular of be occurs well-nigh universally in the UM as wasn't /wʌzənt/ or, occasionally, in uncontracted was not /wəz nat/.

Of the older variants found by Atwood in the East, and less frequently by Virginia McDavid in the North Central region, only two feebly survive as relics in the UM. The assimilated form /wʌdənt/ appears in the speech of four scattered Type I infs.: cvr146; c225; 309, 311. In addition, warn't occurs in the conversation of a Type I Minnesota housewife: "'Twarn't /twɚnt/ good" and "I warn't /wɚnt/ through." All other infs. are reported with wasn't except the few with no record of this item: 25, 37, 42; 117, 125, 151; 208; 305-7; 412.

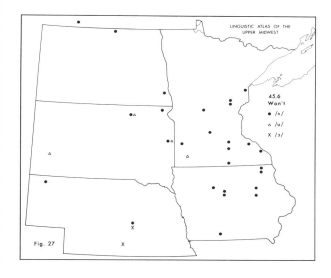

Fig. 27

will not

45.6 I won't do it. NE 702. VF 32; F25.

The present-tense negative of will appears in the context above. Except for a

few scattered infs. who offer the full will not and one who offers I'll not, all infs. have examples of contracted will and not, i.e., won't.

Although the great majority of all UM infs. have the pronunciation /wont/ that is common in southern New England and dominant in the North Central states, some regional variation exists. The form /wʌnt/, common elsewhere in New England and New York and thence found in northern Ohio, Michigan, and Wisconsin, survives in Northern speech territory, specifically northern Iowa and Minnesota. Rare eastern /wʊnt/ appears in the speech of four Type I infs. in Minnesota and South Dakota. Southern Pennsylvania /wɔnt/ may only coincidentally be duplicated in the speech of two Nebraska infs. both of whom have Scandinavian-speaking parents. A unique /want/ also turns up in Nebraska.

	Type I	Type II	Type III
/wont/	80%	93%	93%
/wʌnt/	18%	8%	14%
/wʊnt/	4%	0	0
/wɔnt/	2%	0	0

	Mn.	Ia.	N.D.	S.D.	Nb.	Ave.
/wont/	86%	80%	91%	85%	95%	86%
/wʌnt/	18%	16%	13%	12%	5%	14%
/wʊnt/	2%	0	0	12%	0	2%
/wɔnt/	0	0	0	0	14%	1%

will not 14, 57; 103, 111, 138-39, 144, 150; 305, 319. I'll not 101.

won't /wont/ 1-4, c5, 6-10, c11, 12-14, c15-17, 18-19, 21-22, 25-26, 28-32, 35-42, 44-45, 47, 49, 51-54, 57-62, 64-65; 102, 104-6, 109-12, 116-17, 119-33, 135-37, 139-43, 145-50; 202-3, 205-10, c211, 212-13, 215-20, 222-24, 226; 301-2, c303, 304, 306, 308-10, 312-13, c314, 316, 318-21, 323-28; 401-2, c403, 404-12, 414-16, c417, 418-19, 421, c422, 423-37.

/want/ 413.

/wʌnt/ 18, 23-24, 27, 43, 46, 48, 50, c55, 56, 63; 107-8, 113-16, 118, 144; 201, c204, c225; 306-7, 317; c401, 420.

/wʊnt/ c59; c306, :311, 317.

/wɔnt/ 421, 430.

no response 20, 33-34; 134, 151-52; 214, 221; 315, 322.

INFINITIVE AND PRESENT PARTICIPLE

-ing and a-

45.2a She was singing and laughing. NE 420, 671-72; F34.

The present participle was sought in order to determine the incidence of two features: the contrast between the /ɪŋ/ and /ɪn/ endings, and the presence of initial a- /ə/.

Only occasionally are the specific forms singing and laughing actually obtained in the indicated context. The fws. generally recorded as evidence any participle observed in free conversation. Since fw. practice varies greatly, however, between recording only one sought example and listing a number of conversational instances, the statistics given below can be taken only as general indicators. A single recorded instance of singin', for example, does not necessarily mean that the inf. refrains from using singing at other times.

-ing /ɪŋ/ or /ɪn/ ([ɪn] [+n] [ən])
Historically, the alternation between /ɪŋ/ and /ɪn/ derives from the confusion of three Middle English endings: a noun formative in -ing, a verb inflection in -en, and the original participial ending in -ind. Although the participial written form has long been fixed as -ing, both /ɪŋ/ and /ɪn/ (from -ind) persist in speech. (There is no such phenomenon as the school-nurtured myth of "dropping the g.")

The influence of the written form has contributed to its preference in the schools, a choice reflected in its greater frequency among cultured speakers in the eastern and North Central states and in its fifty-fifty status among Type II speakers in eastern New York, southeastern Pennsylvania, and southern New England. Elsewhere /ɪn/ is the majority form for all except the cultured speakers.

In the UM the school injunction not to "drop your g's" is dutifully observed by only three-fourths of the few recorded college graduates; and more than one-half of these also use /+n/. Six out of 10 of the Type II infs. have the standard /ɪŋ/, but nearly seven out of 10 also are recorded with /ɪn/. One-half of the infs. in this group use both forms. Five out of 10 of the Type I infs. have standard /ɪŋ/ at least occasionally, but nearly nine out of 10 are recorded as using /ɪn/. Nearly one-third in this group, then, likewise use both forms. In the UM as a whole slightly more than one-half of the infs. have /ɪŋ/ but more than three-fourths have /ɪn/, with a consequent overlap of the 31% of the total recorded number who use one form or the other at different times. One inf., 428, consistently uses /ɪn/ on participles but carefully says "a driving horse."

Employment of the /ɪn/ suffix is not limited to participles, however. Although

not specifically sought, its occurrence on words that only distantly relate to participial origins is recorded by several fws. Some of the examples are 'mornin''—3; 'He never done any farmin''—21; 'my own livin' to make'—21; 'fillin' station'—117, 423; 'sewin' machine'—225; 'too easy-goin''—301; 'a million-dollar buildin''—314; 'top o' that buildin''—322; 'pancake doin's at Yankton'—325; 'kindlin''—404; 'durin' daylight hours'—409.

Atwood's remark that probably the extension of /ɪn/ is a matter of phonology, rather than of grammar, is borne out by its appearance in the final weakly accented syllable in some words in which -ing is not a suffix but is part of the historical base. An example is pudding, which for inf. 428 is /pʊdn̩/. See also the treatment of nothing and something in Volume 3.

	Type I	Type II	Type III
/ɪŋ/	49%	61%	75%
/ɪn/	87%	68%	67%

	Mn.	Ia.	N.D.	S.D.	Nb.	Ave.
-ing /ɪŋ/	79%	46%	55%	40%	43%	57%
-in' /ɪn/	78%	75%	90%	90%	68%	78%

-ing c2, c7, 12-13, 18, c19-20, c22, 24, 28, c29, c37-38, c40, 41-42, c43-48, c51, 53-54, c55-57, c58-63, 65; c103, cvr112-13, c117, 118, 120, c122-23, c126, 128, 131, c134, 141, c144, c147, 150; c203, c206, c211-12, c214-15, c220-22; 305, c311, c314, c324; c406-7, cvr410, c415, c419, 424, 426, cvr430-31, 432-33, 435.

-in' c1, c3, c5-6, c8, c13, c15, c19, c21-25, c27, c31-32, 34, c37, c40, c42-44, c46-52, c55-63, c65; cvr101, c105, c107, c109, cvr113, cvr115, c117, 118-19, 121, c122-25, c127-28, c130, cvr138, c139-45, 146, c147-48, 149, c152; c201-4, c207, c209, c211-12, c214-18, c220-22, c224-25; c301-6, c309-12, c314-17, c320, c322, c324-25, c327-28; cvr401, c402-5, c407-9, c412-14, cvr416, c417-23, c427-29, c434, c436.

no response 26, 64; 102, 104, 106, 108, 110-11, 114, 116, 129, 136, 151; 205, 208, 210, 219, 223, 226; 307-8, 313, 318-19, 321, 326; 411, 437.

Comment:
Always or usually -ing: 3, 7, 9, 10, 12, 20, 29-30, 33, 40, 42-45, 47, 52-53; 120-31, 144, 149; 201, 203, 213-14, 221; 304, 312, 325-28; 406.
Usually -in': 25, 60-61; 140; 209; 310-11, 314, 322; 401.

The -ing suffix is recorded also in item 20.6 I am going, We are going, They are going; 20.7 Am I going to, Are they going to; 21.2 I am not going to hurt him; 21.4 We were going to do it; and sometimes in 6.3 The wind is going down, and 61.5 He is going with her. The general picture these additional data provide is not greatly different from the situation described above, except that in the position before /t/, as in going to, a greater range of phonetic variation occurs as the result of assimilation, ranging even in the speech of one individual from slow and formal /goɪŋ tə/ through /go+ntə/ and /gontə/ to rapid and unstressed very informal /gənə/. It is clear that typically /ɪŋ/ is more likely to occur in the speech of Type III speakers than of Type II, and that of Type II than of Type I. It is also clear that, conversely, the /ɪn/ and, particularly, the /gontə/ and /gənə/ forms are more likely to occur in the speech of the less educated. The variants /gonə/ and /gənə/, for example, are found in the field data in the responses of 17% of the Type I infs., 10% of the Type II infs., but none of the Type III's. But such figures are misleading when an item occurs only incidentally and is not specifically sought. Any individual's range is so wide that precise indication of proportions of the several variants cannot be justified by the inadequate field data.

There are no examples of eastern /gwaɪn/.

a- /ə/
Some examples of a-singing and a-laughing were recorded, but most instances of initial a- were observed on other verbs employed in free conversation. Strictly speaking, the verb form here is not a participle but is rather a gerund used as a verbal substantive, the object of a preposition. A- is a weakened form of the preposition on.

This use of a- is found in New England and is characteristic of more than onehalf of the Type I and Type II infs. in the Middle Atlantic states and of more than one-third of those in the North Central region. It is rare, however, among the cultured speakers of Type III.

The UM picture is a fading reflection of that in the eastern and North Central states. The regional distribution of a- seems to be Midland-oriented, with its greater frequency in Iowa, Nebraska, and South Dakota. But although a- is still more common among the least educated, its incidence even in that group has dropped to one-third and in Type II to only onetenth. A lone cultured speaker, an Iowa office secretary, has it in the term a-

singing. The a- prefix is probably on the way toward obsolescence.

a-	Type I 37%	Type II 12%	Type III 6%		

a-	Mn. 15%	Ia. 37%	N.D. 8%	S.D. 29%	Nb. 30%	Ave. 24%

a- c6, c8, c22, 25, c27, c31, 36, c48, c55, c57, 60; 101, c103, c105, c107, c109, c112, cvrl13, c115, c117, 118, 121, cvr132, c133, c135, 137, c139, *146, 147, 150; c206, c220; c304, cvr311, c314, c316-17, c320, c322, 327; cvr401, c403, c405, c407, c414, c422-23, cvr427, cvr429, c434, c436.

to tell

61.2 He came over to tell me about it. NE 572. VF 34.

The infinitive of purpose is recorded in the indicated or a similar context.

Two responses occur. Almost universal in the UM is the simple to tell. The older for to tell is a minor old-fashioned variant in New England and New York but more common in the Middle Atlantic states and still viable in the North Central Atlas region with 112 Type I and II users among 421 infs. This form, however, barely survived the trans-Mississippi migration. Only 11 UM speakers have for to tell, nearly all in Minnesota: c5, 8, c15-16, c21, c25, c40, c48, c56; c139; 429; and all but two, 8 and 40, in Type I.

PHRASES

shall/will

61.3 I shall be disappointed. NE 694.

The future phrase with singular subject is recorded in the indicated or a similar context.

Not sought in the Middle Atlantic survey, this item yielded contrasting data in New England and the North Central states. In northern New England I shall dominates I will and I'll by a ratio of 7:4. But in southeastern New England shall and will are in equal proportions, and in south central and southwestern New England the will forms predominate in a proportion of 2:1. The position of shall is still weaker in the North Central region, where only 10 instances appear, five of them in Ohio and all of them from Types I and II infs.

In the UM the school-taught rule favoring shall is observed by a Type I inf. in Iowa and, in the negative shan't, by a Type II speaker in Nebraska. All other recorded infs. have I'll or, less frequently, I will.

I'll /aɪl/ 1-3, c4-5, 6, c7, c10, 11-12, c13, c15, 18, c19, 20, c21, 22-24, c25, 26-28, 30, c32-33, c35, 36-37, c38, 39-41, c42-47, 48, c49, 50, c51-52, 54-58, c59-63, 64-65; 102, 105, 108-12, 114-15, c116, 117, 119, 121-37, 139, 142-45, 149; 206, c211, 212, 214, c216, 218-19, c220, 222, c225; 301, c302, 303-4, 306-7, 310, c311-13, 315, c320, 321, 324-25, c326, 327-28; c401, 402, c404, 405, c406, 407, 410, 412, 417, c418-19, 429, 437.
I shall /ʃæl/ 140, f147. I shan't /ʃænt/ c414.
I will c52-53; 101, 103-4, 106-7, 113, 138, 141, 146, 148, f149, 150; c201, 213, c219; c302, c312, 318; 413, 415, 420, sn421, 422-28, 431-35.
no response 9, 14, 16-17, 29, 31, 34; 118, 120, 151-52; 202-5, 207-10, 215, 217, 221, 223-24, 226; 305, 308, 314, 316-17, 319, 322-23; 403, 408-9, 411, 416, 430, 436.

61.4 We shall be disappointed. NE 694.

The future phrase with plural subject occurs with distribution and frequency like that with a singular subject.

In the UM all recorded instances are of majority we'll or of less common we will. We shall is given by one Type I Nebraska inf.

we'll /wɪl/ 1, 3-6, c7, 8, c10, 11, c13, 20, 22-28, 30, 32-33, 37-38, 41, c42-43, 44, c45-47, 48-49, c51-53, 54-58, c60-63, 64-65; 101-2, 105, c107, 108-11, 114-15, c116, 117, 119-33, 135, 137, 139, 142, 144-45; 206, c211, 212, 214, 216, 218-20, 222; 301-4, 310, c313, 315, 320-21, 324-26; 401-2, 405, c406, c409, 410, 412, 414, 416-17, c418-19, 429, 433, 437.
we shall /ʃæl/ 434.
we will /wɪl/ 36, 39, 40, 50; 103-4, 106, 112-13, 134, 138, 140-41, 146-48, f149, 150; 318-19; 413, 415, 420, sn421, 422-28, 431-32, s433, 435.
no response 2, 9, 12, 14-19, 21, 29, 31, 34-35, 59; 118, 136, 143, 151-52; 201-5, 207-10, 213, 215, 217, 221, 223-26; 305-9, 311-12, 314, 316-17, 322-23, 327-28; 403-4, 407-8, 411, 430, 436.

done (worked)

45.4 I done worked all day.

This item was added to the North Central worksheets to determine the spread of Southern and South Midland done used as a completive verb with a past participle. It was ascertained as occurring in that area, but with more than two-thirds of the examples provided by old-fashioned speakers in Kentucky.

In the UM only one bona fide instance appears, in the conversational "I done never heard it" of a Type I South Dakota farmer of South Midland parentage, inf. 314. Upon suggestion, however, two Minnesotans, 39 and 48, declared that they had heard it as an old-fashioned form somewhere, the former volunteering that it is "improper."

might could

74.8 He might be able to do it. VF 35; F28, F31.

Added to the UM worksheets near the end of the Minnesota fieldwork, this item is intended to ascertain the spread of might could, which in the East occurs in the South and South Midland and also in the Pennsylvania German part of south central Pennsylvania. In the North Central states might could is largely a Type I form found in Kentucky.

In the UM might could occurs in the speech of seven scattered Type I infs. and one Type II. Only three of the eight have South Midland family backgrounds. Because the item turned out to be so unproductive, fws. tended to pass over it, but a more persistent effort in Nebraska might have yielded further instances.

might be able to 30; 101-4, sn105, 106, sn107, 108-12, 114-17, 119-42, 144-49, sn150, sn152; 201-5, 208, 210-15, 217-21; 309-13, 319-20, 322-26; 401, 404, 406, 408, 410-12, 418-19, 429, 436-37.
might could sn35; 113, 143; [1]205, c209, sn216, sn223-24; [1]311; 402.
no response 1-29, 31-34, 36-65; 118, 151; 206-7, 222, 225-26; 301-8, 314-18, 321, 327-28; 403, 405, 407, 409, 413-17, 420-28, 430-35.

Comment:
might could: Inf. has heard this used by a person who moved here from Ill.—205.

CHAPTER 3

Nouns

PLURALS

hoofs

28.4 <u>hoofs</u>.

Although the historical plural <u>hooves</u> /huvz/ or /hʊvz/ has largely given way to widespread analogical <u>hoofs</u> /hufs/ or /hʊfs/, it still persists despite the assertion of Bergen Evans in his *Dictionary of Contemporary American Usage*: "The old plural *hooves* is now used only in poetry."

Actually <u>hooves</u> is the customary form for nearly one-fifth of the UM infs., but, as the accompanying map indicates, it has not spread into the more recently settled western portions. It has been retained chiefly by Type II speakers.

<u>Hoofs</u> is the dominant form throughout the UM. For the pronunciation variants see Volume 3.

Inf. 35 has an analogous <u>loafs</u> for <u>loaves</u>.

	Type I	Type II	Type III
hoofs	89%	75%	81%
hooves	11%	25%	19%

	Mn.	Ia.	N.D.	S.D.	Nb.	Ave.
hoofs	79%	86%	96%	93%	65%	82%
hooves	21%	14%	4%	7%	35%	18%

hoofs /fs/ 1, 3-4, c5, 6-11, 13-17, !18, 19-25, 27-29, 31, 33-36, 38-39, 41-44, 46, 48-51, 54, 56-60, 63, 65; 101, 103, 105-15, 117-23, 126, :127-28, 129-30, 132-35, 137-51; 201-21, 223-26; 301-5, 307-12, 314-26, 328; c401, 402-3, 405-12, 415-18, 421, 425, 427, 429-32, 435-36.

hooves /vz/ 2, 12, 26, 30, 32, 37, 40, 45, 47, 52-53, 61-62; 102, 104, 116, 125, 131, 136, 152; 222; 306, 313; c404, 413-14, :419, 420, 422-24, 426, 428, 433-34, 437.

no response 55, 64; 124; 327.

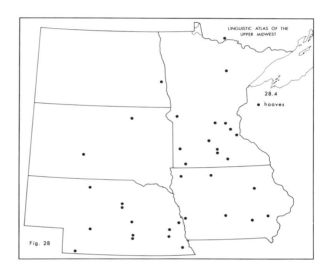

Fig. 28

28.4
• hooves

LINGUISTIC ATLAS OF THE UPPER MIDWEST

Comment:
 <u>hoofs</u>: "'Hooves' would be forced"—33.

horseshoe(s)

28.3 <u>horseshoe</u>(s). NE 199.

Following the expression "play" or "pitch (a game of)" both the singular and the plural forms of <u>horseshoe</u> occur.

In New England only 15 scattered older infs., about 3%, have the singular, but in the UM the singular is the majority form in Midland speech territory and is used by one-third of the infs. in Minnesota and by one-half of those in North Dakota. It may be receding in favor of the plural form, however, since it is used by a greater proportion of recorded Type I infs. than by Type II's.

	Type I	Type II	Type III
horseshoe	57%	49%	37%
horseshoes	32%	47%	63%

	Mn.	Ia.	N.D.	S.D.	Nb.	Ave.
horseshoe	31%	65%	50%	67%	62%	52%
horseshoes	52%	33%	42%	33%	38%	41%

For individual responses see this item in Volume 1.

houses

11.3 <u>houses</u>.

Sought in the Middle Atlantic survey but not in New England, the plural of house is revealed in the UM field data as having a minor analogical variant in which the s of the base, historically voiced as in /hauzɪz/, is voiceless, as in /hausɪz/.

The UM typically has the form with /z/, but 13 scattered infs. have simple /hausɪz/: four Type I's, seven Type II's, and two Type III's. No clear regional or social pattern emerges. Those with /s/ are 9, 28, 41, *60; 131, 134, 149; 206, 214, 216; 430, 436-37.

moths

47.1 <u>moths</u>. NE 236.

The plural of <u>moth</u> is usually either /mɔðz/ or /mɔθs/.

In New England historical /mɔðz/ dominates the second form. A few infs. there have simple /mɔz/ and two have <u>moth</u> as both singular and plural.

In the UM the voiced /mɔðz/ is likewise the over-all majority choice, but only because of its strength in Midland-oriented Iowa, South Dakota, and Nebraska; voiceless /mɔθs/ dominates in Minnesota and North Dakota. As in New England, the /ðz/ is too much for a few scattered infs. (17, 45, 59; 104; 322, 327; 401-2), who solve their problem by reducing the form to /mɔz/, while some others, mostly in southern Iowa, are content with simple <u>moth</u> as both singular and plural: 109, 122, 124, 134, 136, 140, 143, 146; 225; 327.

The UM Midland orientation of the voiced /ðz/ plural does not, however, seem to reflect a more widespread similar orientation, since Wisconsin, a Northern state, has a higher proportion of infs. having the voiced plural than does Illinois, nearly all of which is Midland. In Wisconsin there are 16 instances of the voiced plural in contrast with 30 of the voiceless. In Illinois, according to data privately provided by McDavid, only 12 infs. have the voiced plural (one /ðz/ and 11 /z/) in contrast with 37 having the voiceless /θs/.

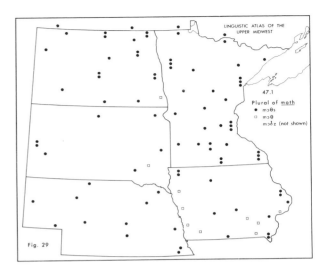

Fig. 29

47.1
Plural of <u>moth</u>
● mɔθs
□ mɔθ
mɔðz (not shown)

LINGUISTIC ATLAS OF THE
UPPER MIDWEST

But the uninflected plural of southern Iowa, ending in simple /θ/, does seem to be Midland, since only three out of 50 infs. in Wisconsin have this form, in contrast with 11 out of 59 in Illinois.

	Type I	Type II	Type III
-/s/	50%	40%	44%
-/z/	45%	58%	50%

	Mn.	Ia.	N.D.	S.D.	Nb.	Ave.
-/s/	55%	26%	73%	27%	47%	44%
-/z/	46%	59%	23%	73%	54%	50%

-/s/ 1-10, 12-13, 15-16, 18-19, 23, 26-27, 34-38, 43, 47-48, 50-51, 53, 56-58, 62, 64-65; 101-2, 112, 120-21, 123, 126, 129, 138-39, 145, 148-49; 201-9, 211-13, 215-17, 220-21, 223-24; 303, 307, 309-11, 318, 323; 403, 407-9, 412, 415, 417-18, 421, 423, 428, 431-32, 435-36.

-/z/ 11-12, 14, 17, 21, 25, 29-33, 39-42, 44-46, 48-49, 52, 54, 59-61, 63; 103-8, 110-11, 113-19, 125, 127-28, 130-33, 135, 137, 141-42, 144, 147, 150, 152; 210, 214, 218-19, 222, 226; 301-2, 304, 308, 312-17, 319-22, 324-28; 401-2, 404, 406, 410-11, 413, 416, 419-20, 424-27, 429-30, 433, 437.

no response 122, 143, 151; 225; 305-6; 414, 422.

shafts

17.5 <u>shafts</u> (for a buggy). NE 171.

Of the words gleaned for this item (see Volume 1), <u>shafts</u> is the most common. Although ignored by current commercial dictionaries except those in the G. & C. Merriam series, the dominant pronunciation of the plural in New England is /ʃævz/, with voiceless /ʃæfts/ or /ʃæfs/

48

only minority alternates and then particularly in the western portion of Massachusetts and Connecticut.

In the UM 169 (85%) of the responding
infs. use <u>shafts</u> rather than <u>fills</u> or
<u>thrills</u>. Of this number slightly more
than half, mostly in Type I and Type II,
have the voiced plural /ʃævz/. A regional
weighting appears in the higher proportion in Iowa and Nebraska, Midland speech
territory. A possible trend toward
/ʃæfts/ is now unlikely to develop in
view of the obsolescence of the referent.
Not very many young people have occasion
to talk about horse-drawn vehicles.

The percentages given below refer to
the number of infs. replying with some
form of <u>shafts</u>.

	Type I	Type II	Type III
/ʃæfts/	44%	47%	81%
/ʃævz/	56%	53%	19%

	Mn.	Ia.	N.D.	S.D.	Nb.	Ave.
/ʃæfts/	64%	28%	50%	58%	46%	48%
/ʃævz/	36%	72%	50%	42%	54%	52%

/ʃæfts/ 1-7, 11, 14-15, 17-20, 24, 28-
29, 32, 34, 37, 39-40, 45-47, 51, 53, 58,
*60, 62; 108, 121, 123, 126, 128-29, 131,
*134, 140-41, 144, 149, 150-51; 201-3,
206, 217, 219-22, 224; 308-13, 316, 321,
323-26; 402-3, 407-10, 412-15, 417, 422,
424-26, 431-32.

/ʃævz/ 8, 10, 12-13, 21, 25, 30-31, 35-
36, 43-44, 49, 54, 57, 60-61; 101-2, 104,
109, 111-15, 117-20, 122, 124-25, 127,
130, 132-33, 135-39, 141-43, 145-46; 204-
5, 207-9, 211-15, 218; 301-3, 306, 315-
16, 318, 320, 322; 401, 404-5, 411, 416,
418-21, 423, 427-30, 433-37.

troughs

10.3 eavestroughs.
29.5 (hog/pig)troughs. NE 208.

The plural of <u>trough</u> is usually recorded in 10.3, as part of the compound
<u>eavestroughs</u>, but sometimes in 29.5, ei-
ther as a simple form or as a member of
such compounds as <u>pigtroughs</u> or <u>hog-
troughs</u>.

In New England the more common singular
is <u>troth</u>, with voiceless /θ/, which
yields a voiced plural /trɔðz/ more frequently than it does the voiceless
/trɔθs/. Plurals in /fs/ and /vz/ are
less common; quite rare are /trɔz/ and
the uninflected /trɔð/ or /trɔ/, the second of which is found in southwestern New
England. A very few infs. have a singular
/trɔθ/ contrasting with a plural in either /fs/ or /vz/.

A curiously contrasting situation ap-

pears in the North Central states, however, if evidence from Wisconsin and Illinois, the two states adjoining the UM,
represents the region as a whole. In Wisconsin, the majority of the informants,
actually three-fourths, have a voiceless
plural rather than one in either /ðz/ or
/vz/. In Illinois, according to data provided by McDavid, five-sixths of the
infs. have /θs/ or /fs/; only one-sixth
have a voiced plural. Neither state af-
fords instances of the eastern minority
forms /trɔð/ and /trɔ/.

But this apparent trend toward loss of
the historical plural in /z/ is not supported by the data in the UM. In North-
ern-oriented Minnesota and North and
South Dakota the dominant plural is likewise the voiceless /s/, but in Midland-
oriented Iowa and Nebraska the /z/ plural
apparently has experienced new vitality,
for here, as in the East, it is again, by
a slight margin, the principal variant.

All UM infs. recorded with voiceless
/s/ have /trɔfs/ except these scattered
ones with /trɔθs/: 9, 57, 65; 305-6, 313;
407. Of those with the voiced plural all
have /trɔvz/ except the following, who
have /trɔðz/: 11; 107, 110, 117, 135,
146; 205, 218, 226; 308, 316-17; 401,
405, 408, 426. No uninflected plurals appear.

A rather clear trend is a reduction to
two forms, /fs/ and /vz/, with a possible
further reduction to only the regular
/fs/. The ambivalence found during such a
process appears with those infs. who alternate between voiced and voiceless
forms: 10, 21; 114, 147; 306, 326; 406,
428, 435.

	Type I	Type II	Type III
-/s/	61%	71%	64%
-/z/	44%	39%	43%

	Mn.	Ia.	N.D.	S.D.	Nb.	Ave.
-/s/	93%	41%	62%	68%	37%	65%
-/z/	12%	63%	38%	46%	54%	42%

-/s/ 1-5, 7-10, 13-18, 20-29, 31, 33-
35, 38, 40-45, 47, 49-50, 52, 55, 57, 62,
64-65; 102, 106, 109, 114, 117, 123, 126,
128-30, 134, 138, 147, 149-52; 202-4,
206-7, 209, 211-13, 215-17, 219-20, 223,
225; 301-7, 309-15, 319, 321, 323, 326-
27; 402-3, 406-7, 409, 411-12, 415-19,
423, 428, 430-33, 435-37.

-/z/ 10-12, 17, 21, 30; 101, 103-5,
107, 111-13, 115-18, 122, 124-25, 131-33,
135, 137, 139, 142-43, 145-47, 149; 201,
205, 208, 210, 214, 218, 221-22, 224,
226; 302, 306, 308, 315-18, 320, 322,
324-26, 328; 401, 404-6, 408, 410, 413-
14, 420-29, 434-35.

no response 6, 19, 32, 36-37, 39, 46,

48, 51, 53-54, 56, 58-61, 63; 108, 110, 119-21, 127, 136, 140-41, 144, 148.

way(s)

33.1 a little way over there.
33.2 a long way to go. NE 48, 50-51.

Ways in such contexts as those above, where it is commonly construed as plural, probably is really singular in origin, with its source the Middle English genitive. Because of the conflict between an apparently plural form and a singular meaning, however, schools have tended to favor the use of way without conspicuous success.

In New England ways is dominant among all speakers, despite strong competition from way in Massachusetts, Rhode Island, and Connecticut.

Ways is similarly dominant among the three groups throughout the UM. It is used by more than eight out of 10 infs., but some of them also use way, particularly in Type II and Type III groups. A few speakers vary in their choice according to the semantic context. The following have a little ways but a long way: 4, 14; 122, 126, 141, 145; 423, 431-33, 437. Some other infs. reverse the choice by having a little way but a long ways: 11, 65; 220; 406, 427, 435.

	Type I	Type II	Type III
way	24%	30%	47%
ways	86%	82%	73%

	Mn.	Ia.	N.D.	S.D.	Nb.	Ave.
way	26%	25%	19%	19%	46%	28%
ways	80%	80%	85%	85%	92%	84%

Because this item was primarily aimed at the lexical contrast between way and piece or distance, it was also included in the mailed checklist (see Volume 1). Although the returns reveal ways dominance, there is a higher incidence of way than in the field data, a fact that may point to a weakness in a mail survey for a grammatical matter. A person who habitually uses ways may well circle way on a printed checklist because he feels that it is the "correct" form and thinks that he might use it at least once in a while. The checklist responses total 1040, proportioned as follows:

	Mn.	Ia.	N.D.	S.D.	Nb.	Ave.
way	46%	45%	39%	48%	41%	44%
ways	53%	51%	63%	54%	59%	55%

way 3-4, 11-12, 14, 18, 22, 26, 28-29, 32-33, 42, c44, 46, 61, 65; 109-11, 113, 122, 126, 129-31, 133, 141, 145, 149; 203, 214, 222; 306, 310, 315-16, 318; 401, 406, 409-10, 412, 420, 422-24, 426-28, 431-33, 435, 437.

ways 1-2, 4-5, c6-7, 8-9, c10-11, 12-14, c15, c19, 20-21, 23-25, 27, 30-31, 34-36, 38-39, c40, 41, 43, 45, 47-50, c51, 52-59, cr60, 62-64, c65; 102-4, 106-9, 112, 114-18, c119, 121-28, c130, 132, 134-50, 152; c201, 204-5, c206, 207-13, 215, c216, 217-19, c220-21, 223-26; 301, 303-5, 307-9, 312-17, 320-26, c327, 328; c401, 402, c403, 404, c405, 406, cvr407-8, c410, 411, c412, 413-14, c415, 416-19, 421-23, 425-27, cvr428, c429-30, 431-37.

Comment:

long way: Inf. first offered 'ways' but then, calling it "ungrammatical," switched to 'way,' which she had already offered for 33.1-40. "A 'short way' and 'long ways'—those are the two"—65.

PLURALS AFTER NUMERALS

Comparative information from the Atlantic and North Central states cited here is from the study by Raven and Virginia McDavid, "Plurals of nouns of measure in the United States," in *Studies in Languages and Linguistics in Honor of Charles C. Fries*, edited by Albert H. Marckwardt for publication by the English Language Institute of the University of Michigan in 1964.

In the eastern surveys this feature was investigated for year, foot, mile, head (of lettuce), bushel, pound, and yoke. Only the last three of these were retained in the shorter worksheets of the North Central and Upper Midwest atlases.

After numerals all these words occur both in the regular plural and also in what is often interpreted as a singular. The origin of the latter, however, is the Old English genitive plural, the customary grammatical construction following numerals above three, since such numerals were usually considered as nouns rather than as adjectives. Old English *fif fota*, literally "five of feet," historically developed into five foot. The use of the form feet is simply due to the analogy with the plural feet as subject or as object. Other words, such as mile, sometimes followed the same pattern.

bushel(s)

34.3 bushel (pl.). NE 127.

After a numeral, historical bushel as a plural is the usual form for about one-half of the New England and Middle Atlantic infs., including a sprinkling of Type III's. No clear contrast appears between North and Midland, but the uninflected plural is less common in the South Atlantic sector. More than one-half of the North Central infs. choose this form as well, e.g., 65% in Michigan and 52% in Illinois.

In the UM the situation is only slightly different. The proportion in the two northern states, Minnesota and North Dakota, drops to 40%; it is higher in Iowa and Nebraska. This uninflected plural is more characteristic of the speech of the less educated.

	Type I	Type II	Type III
bushel	62%	49%	13%
bushels	43%	52%	87%

	Mn.	Ia.	N.D.	S.D.	Nb.	Ave.
bushel	40%	75%	40%	50%	53%	52%
bushels	62%	26%	64%	54%	50%	50%

bushel 4-5, 9-10, 12, 14, c15, 21-22, c23, 24, c25, 30-31, 40-41, 46-47, c48, c51, 55-56, 60, 63-64; 103-6, 109, 112-14, c115, 116-19, 122, *123, 124-25, 128-30, 132-33, 135-43, 145-49, 152; 204-8, 210, 218, 220, 224, c225; 301, 306-8, 311, 316-18, 320, 322-25; 401-3, c404, 413-14, *417, 420-21, 428-33, cvr434, 436-37.

bushels 1-3, 6, c7, 8, 11, 13, c15, c16, 17-20, 26-28, 32-34, 36-39, 42-45, c49, 50, 52-54, c57, 58-59, 61-62, c65; 101-2, 107-8, 111, 115, 120-21, 126, 131, 134, 144, 150; 201-3, 209, 211-13, 215-17, 219, 221-23, 225-26; 302-5, 309, 312-13, c314, 315, 317, 319, 321, 326, 328; c405, 407-11, 415, c416, 417, !418, 419, 422-26, 435.

no response 29, 35; 110, 127, 151; 214; 310, 327; 406, 412, 427.

pound(s)

36.5 pound (pl.). NE 556.

The McDavids report pound as plural "distributed almost evenly throughout the three major dialect regions of the Atlantic Seaboard." In the North Central states it is most frequent in Indiana and Kentucky. In no states but West Virginia and Indiana is it favored by more than one of the cultivated infs.

In the UM the general frequency of pound as plural is lower than in the other investigated areas. Minnesota's 11% corresponds with Michigan's 11% and Wisconsin's 16%, but Iowa's 8% does not match Illinois's 34% and Ohio's 24%. Nor does the South Midland influence inferred

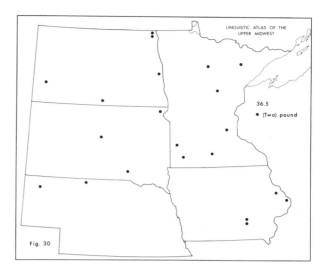

Fig. 30

in Indiana and Kentucky appear in the UM, where the greatest frequency is in North Dakota rather than in Iowa and Nebraska. No Type III speaker uses pound. The normalizing power of books and schools apparently has affected pound much more than it has bushel.

	Type I	Type II	Type III
pound	15%	7%	0
pounds	89%	94%	100%

	Mn.	Ia.	N.D.	S.D.	Nb.	Ave.
pound	11%	8%	19%	11%	5%	10%
pounds	94%	94%	81%	93%	95%	92%

pound 10, c13, 21, cvr37, ¹†40, c46, 53, c59; 121, 135, c136, c139; 207-8, 214, cvr220, 223; 307, c314, 322; c402, 403.

pounds 1-9, 11, c12-16, 17-20, cvr21, 22-34, c35, 36-42, c44, 45, c47, 48-52, 54-55, c56, 57-58, 60-65; 101-20, 122-34, 137-50, 152; 201-6, 209-13, 215-18, c219, 221-22, 224-26; 301-6, 308-10, c311-12, 313, c314, 315-21, 323-26, c327, 328; 401, 404-18, c419, 420-24, c425, 426-29, c430, 431, c432, 433-37.

no response 43; 151.

yoke(s)

27.3 yoke (pl.). NE 189.

To many infs. an ox-yoke and oxen themselves are things of the past, only heard about and not experienced. For them the expression two yoke of oxen is almost a formula, remembered as a whole. No wonder that the uninflected plural yoke has retained majority frequency among all infs. in all investigated areas.

In the North Central states and the Upper Midwest, however, even its historical significance and the remembered expression have receded so far that some less-educated speakers regularize the plural to yokes. No Type III inf. does this. Its usage status, hence, is clearly unlike that of the uninflected plurals of bushel and pound.

No regional pattern appears in the UM except that in the western half, where farming developed largely after the disappearance of oxen, the incidence of yokes increases to 30% from the 20% in Minnesota and Iowa.

The percentages below are of the three types of infs. offering one of the yoke forms.

	Type I	Type II	Type III
yoke	75%	85%	100%
yokes	31%	15%	0

	Mn.	Ia.	N.D.	S.D.	Nb.	Ave.
yoke	86%	81%	69%	88%	67%	80%
yokes	14%	23%	31%	25%	40%	25%

yoke 1, 4, 12, 17-18, cvr19, cr22, c23, c25-26, 29, c30, 32, 40, 43-44, cvr46, 47, 51-53, c56, 57-63, 65; 101, 103, 108, 113, 116, 118-19, 122, 125-26, c129, 130, *134, 137, 142-43, 145-46, 148, 151-52; c202, 205, cr207, 208, 210, 212-13, 216, 218, cr220, 226; c301, c305, 307-8, c309, c312, 313, 315, 317, 319-20, 322, 324, 328; c409, 414, 416, 418, 422-23, 425-26, cr432, 434.
yokes 10, 24, ?28, 37, 39, c54; 105, c112, 114, c124, 129, 135; c201, 206, 214, 223, c225; 301-2, 316, c322; 407, 409, 413, 415, 420, 427.

For 72 infs. historic yoke has been replaced by one of three synonyms, pair, span, and team, but with similar proportions of inflected and uninflected plurals after two.

As with yoke, the users of pair and span strongly prefer the plural without -s, the so-called zero plural. All of those in Types I and III say two pair; so do 57% of the Type II's.

pair 11, 41; c107, 109, 132, 147; 204, 209, 215-16, 221; 306, 319; 421, c426, 428.
pairs †304, 325; 421.

Likewise, five of the six users of span, a term customarily used of horses rather than of oxen, have only the uninflected form after two.

span 45, 53; 139; c202; 323.
spans 34.

But team, a word also usually associated with horses rather than with oxen, reveals a much greater impact of the tendency toward regularization. Although exactly 50% of the older and less-educated users retain simple team as a plural, 62% of the high school group have gone to the inflected form with -s, as have all of the Type III's. The regularizing thrust is consistent here with its manifestation in the distribution of verb forms, as it is stronger in the three western states with 70% teams than in Minnesota and Iowa, with 46% teams.

team 1, 2, 5, 19-20, 25, 31, 35, c36, 48, 55; 107, 118, 120; c208, 224; 318, c327; 417, 433.
teams 3, 18, 27, 33; 42, 44, 49-50; 104, 120-21, 139; 203, 217; 303, c314, 316; †401, c403, 405, 421-22, 424, 429, c430, 435.

CHAPTER 4

Pronouns

PLURALS

you

35.2 When are <u>you</u> coming again?

The singular and plural second-person pronominal forms are recorded in the context above or in some other suitable one.

Throughout the UM <u>you</u> with plural meaning is the accepted form, but a desire for differentiating singular and plural appears in the variants a few infs. offer.

Nonstandard <u>youse</u>, usually assigned to Northern American English, is offered by two Type I infs. (c204; 432), one with English parents and the other with one Irish parent.

Nonstandard <u>you-uns</u>, typically found in eastern Midland, does not occur at all.

<u>You-all</u>, a South Midland and Southern form, is used by 10 infs. (40; 104-5, 133, 139; 317; 409, 428, 430-31), most of them with South Midland antecedents or in an area of some South Midland influence. But the Minnesota inf., with a distinct /juɔɪ/ which she was embarrassed to admit using, probably is not using the South Midland /jɔɪ/. Although <u>you-all</u> is common with both educated and uneducated speakers in the South, no Type III speakers in the UM say it and only three Type II speakers (40; 105; 428), in contrast with seven in Type I (104; 133, 139; 317; 409, 430-31). Infs. 409 and 429 assert that their use, however, is humorous. Inf. 312 volunteers that he dislikes the form.

Of the other locutions devised to distinguish a plural, <u>you folks</u> is widespread. It is used only by Type I infs. (c15; 101, 103, 114, 132, 137; 212; 415—as <u>you folk</u>) and by Type II infs. (57;

102, 106, 115, 121, 138; c203; 430). Actually, this form may be much more prevalent, since fw. A did not record this form when it was offered.

Two infs. have the phrase <u>you people</u> (113; 413).

who

35.3 <u>Who-all</u> was/were there?

For the plural of the interrogative pronoun more than one-half of the UM infs. use the phrase <u>who-all</u>; slightly less than one-half have no distinctive plural of any kind.

Despite the high frequency of <u>who-all</u> in North Dakota, the drop in the proportion between Iowa and Minnesota, and between Nebraska and South Dakota, strongly suggests that this form has Midland orientation.

No sharp social contrasts appear, although Type II infs. favor <u>who-all</u> more than do those in the two other groups.

	Type I	Type II	Type III
who	44%	46%	50%
who-all	58%	70%	50%

	Mn.	Ia.	N.D.	S.D.	Nb.	Ave.
who	62%	44%	35%	54%	22%	45%
who-all	43%	66%	77%	58%	84%	58%

who 1, 5, 9-10, 12, c15-16, 17-18, 20, 23, 26-28, c29, :30, 31-32, 34-40, 44-45, 47-49, 51-54, 57, f59, 61-63; 102-12, 116, 119-20, 123, 129, 132, 134, 138, 140, 142, 146; 201, 208, 210-11, 215-17, 219, 226; 301, 304, 306-8, 312-16, 319, 324, 326; 408, sn409, 411, 415-16, 418, 427, 436.

who all [1]1, 2-3, sn4, [1]7, sn8, c11, [1]20, 21, sn22, sn24, 25, sn30, 31, 33, *37, 41, [1]42, 43, !46, [1]47, 50, 53, sn54-55, 56-57, s[1]58, 60, c*60, 63-64, sn65;

101, c102, 104, s105, s108, s110-11, 113-18, 121-22, 124, sn125, 126-28, 130-31, s132, 133, *134, 135-39, 141, 143-45, 147-50; 202-6, sn207, sn209-10, sn212, 213-14, sn215, 218, sn220, 221-25, sn226; 301-3, sn304, 310, 317-18, ¹319, 320-23, s324, 325-26, 328; sn401, 402, sn403, 404, :405, 406-7, *408, 410, sn412, 413-14, 417, 419-23, sn424, 425, sn426, 428, c429, 430-33, sn434, 435, sn436, 437.

no response 6, 13-14, 19; 151-52; 305, 309, 311, 327.

Comment:
who-all: "That'd be the proper word"—25. "Who-all is Southern"—34.

what

35.4 What(-all) did he say?

For the plural or inclusive meaning of the neuter interrogative pronoun most UM infs. have no distinctive form. More than one-third, however, use the phrase what-all. As with you-all, the somewhat higher frequency in North Dakota does not accord with the inference, clearly implied by the more than two-thirds majority in Nebraska, that what-all may be Midland-oriented.

	Type I	Type II	Type III
what	73%	64%	69%
what-all	28%	48%	25%

	Mn.	Ia.	N.D.	S.D.	Nb.	Ave.
what	64%	72%	65%	75%	53%	69%
what-all	30%	32%	35%	29%	65%	37%

what 1, 3, 5-6, 9, 11-14, c15, 17-18, 21, 23, 26-29, :30, 32-41, 43-45, fn46, 47-49, 51-54, 56-57, f59, 60, 62-63; 101-17, 119-23, 126-27, 129, 132-33, 135, 138-39, 141-42, 144-46, 149; 202, 205-7, 209-14, 216-17, 219-22, 224; 303, 305-8, 312-20, 323, 325-26, 328; 402, 404, 408-9, 411, 413, 416, sn417, 418-19, 421-22, 425, 427-28, 432, 436-37.

what-all 2, 4, sn8, sn10, c14, c16, 20, ¹21, 22, sn24, 25, sn26, sn30, sn31, s¹42, fn46, ¹47, 50, ¹53, sn54, ¹58, 60, c*60, 61, ¹65; s105, 117-18, 124, sn125, 128, 130-31, 134, 136-37, s138, 140, 143, 147-50; 201, 203-4, 208, sn215, 218, 223, sn225-26; 301-2, sn304, 310, sn320, 321-22; sn402-4, :405, 406-7, sn410, c412, 414, sn419, 420-21, 423, 426, 429-31, 433-35, sn436-37.

no response 7, 19, 55, 64; 151-52; 309, 311, 324, 327; 401, 415, 424.

Comment:
what-all: "Better" than 'what'—46. "If we wanted to be sure we got it all"—149.

GENITIVES

ours/yours

34.7 It's ours/yours. NE 615.

The forms ourn and yourn were still fairly common among older and less-educated infs. in Connecticut and western Massachusetts west of the Berkshires, as well as in southern New Hampshire, at the time of the New England survey. But in the UM the normalizing power of the schools apparently has extinguished ourn and left only faint embers of yourn in the records of 13 infs. Two of these—48 and 114—are recorded as using yourn in conversation. Four—22, 39, 40, and 42—admit to having used yourn at one time but now consider it old-fashioned or wrong. Seven—1, 6, 34, 49, 57, 64, and 136—simply say that they have heard it but do not use it themselves. The distribution suggests a Northern orientation for the -n form, but evidence from the Middle Atlantic and North Central studies may indicate otherwise. Yours is common with all UM groups and ours is their unanimous choice.

his/hers/theirs

35.1 It's his/hers. NE 616. It's theirs. NE 617.

The -n forms, hisn, hern, theirn, of these genitives have in New England a distribution like that of ourn and yourn, except that theirn is more sparsely represented in Connecticut. Standard his, hers, and theirs are widespread.

In the UM the -n forms survive largely as remembered or locally heard. They are clearly nonstandard relics.

Hisn is actually a customary form for only five UM infs.—sn27, 118, c132, *223, and 422; hern and theirn occur in the observed speech of only one inf.—c114. Several infs. identify hisn as obsolescent—!⌐†31, s†39, †40, s†48, ⌐†50, †65; and so do some with respect to hern and theirn—s†39, s†48, ⌐†50. Inf. 50 says that his grandmother used all three forms. Inf. 27 comments about his and hisn, "Both is right," but inf. 65 calls hisn a "bad" term.

you/who/what/-all's

35.2 you-all's.
35.3 who-all's.
35.4 what-all's.

Attempts to elicit a genitive for the compound plurals in -all proved fruitless except for who-all's. Four infs., three of them in the Midland speech zone, have this genitive—50; 310, 321, 328. One, s424, accepts it as suggested, admitting that she uses it even though it does not seem "natural"; two more—s108 and s402—accept it but probably do not use it themselves. One, 326, has heard it from others.

RELATIVES

who/that

41.6 He's the man who owns the orchard. NE 629.

Although orchard was included in the key sentence for its phonetic value, the difficulty experienced by fws. in eliciting it in a region without orchards led to their accepting any reasonable noun, e.g., garage, hardware store, or hotel.

The primary function of this item is the determination of the relative pronoun having a personal antecedent and used as subject in a contained restrictive clause. Two forms are usual, who and that, in addition to that he, what, he, and the omission of any form at all.

In New England that predominates throughout, but who is a close second in the southern half, though infrequent in Vermont, New Hampshire, and Maine. That he occurs but once, on Cape Cod. The over-all frequency of the omitted rela-

tive is nearly 9%, but more than two-thirds of the instances are in the northern half of New England.

In the UM that also is dominant, with two-thirds of the infs. using it in preference to who. No regional pattern emerges, but there is a clear social contrast in the progressively higher proportion of who on the range from the infs. with less education to those with more education.

The redundant that he turns up three times in the following instances recorded in the free speech of Type I infs.: "They had a caller there that he got $600 for callin' one night"—c225. "I have a grandson that he is the fourth . . ."—c409. "I worked with a man that he had his horses . . ."—c418.

What, not recorded in New England, is offered by three UM infs. There are no examples of as. He occurs once.

The omitted relative is recorded for 6% of the UM speakers, a figure comparable to 7% in Wisconsin. This feature may have Northern orientation, but its nonoccurrence in Iowa could be a result of fw. practice. It does appear with sharp social contrast, as a minor syntactic marker in the speech of eight Type I infs. and two Type II's. The examples, all but two in free conversation, are as follows: "That's the man runs the store"—1. "We had one cow would . . ."—c15. ". . . stayed with people were rich"—c16. "He's the man owns the hotel"—26. "There was a woman once come to see me"—c45. "I have shoes go back before the Civil War"—cvr51. "There's always something interesting happens"—cvr60. "There was a man wrote a book about the Black Hills"—c314. "There was a boy had run away . . ."—cvr327. "One time there was a preacher come there . . ."—c403.

	Type I	Type II	Type III
that	77%	65%	27%
who	19%	42%	73%
"omitted"	10%	2%	0

	Mn.	Ia.	N.D.	S.D.	Nb.	Ave.
that	70%	69%	62%	67%	68%	68%
who	31%	31%	35%	29%	41%	33%
"omitted"	13%	0	4%	7%	3%	6%

he c16.

that 4, 6-8, c10, 11-12, c13, 14, c17-18, c21, c23, 24-25, sn28, c30-31, 32, sn35, 36-41, cvr42, 43-45, 48, 51-52, cvr54, 55-57, 59-60, cvr61, 63-64, c65; 101, 104-9, 112-15, 117, 119-22, 124, 127-29, 132-35, 138-43, 146-49; 201, c203, 206-9, sn210, 211-12, 215-16, 218-20, 223-24; c301, 303-8, 311, c312, 316-18, c320, 321-23, 325-26; 401, c404, 405-8, c412, cvr413, c414, 415, cvr416, 417,

419-20, c422, 424, cvr427, c428, 429,
c430, cvr431, 434-37.
   that he 225; c409, c418.
   what c44, c48; c415.
   who 2-3, 5, 9-10, 12, c13, 20, 33-34,
42, 46-47, 49-50, 53, 58, 62, 65; 102-3,
110-11, 116, 118, 123, 125-26, 130-31,
136-37, 144-45; 202, 205, 213-14, 216-
17, 221-22, 226; 302, 309-10, c312, 313,
319, 324, sn328; 402, 409-11, c414, 421,
c422, 423, c425, 426, c428, 431-33, 437.
   relative pronoun omitted 1, c13, c15-
16, 26, c45, cvr51, cvr60; 204; c314,
cvr327; c403.
   no response 19, 22, 27, 29; 150-52;
315.

whose

41.7 He is a boy <u>whose</u> father is very
rich. NE 651.

Most infs. solve the problem of embed-
ding a clause with a possessive refer-
ential relation by using the relative
<u>whose</u>. This is true in New England,
though its proportional frequency is
lower in Maine, Vermont, and New Hampshire. It is also true in the UM, where
no clear regional contrast appears,
since about two-thirds of the infs. in
each state offer it. The slightly lower
frequency in Nebraska and the mere 29%
frequency in southern Iowa (possibly due
to fw. practice?) might indicate a lower
incidence of <u>whose</u> in Midland speech, but
confirmation of such a guess must be
sought in the still unpublished North
Central and Middle Atlantic atlas materials.
   Many persons, however, especially the
less educated, find <u>whose</u> too difficult
to handle and either resort to various
unorthodox equivalents or give up com-
pletely, like 220 and 424, with such a
comment as "I don't know how you would
say that."
   Both in New England and in the UM the
most frequent equivalent in a context
with a masculine antecedent is <u>that his</u>.
Nearly one-third of the Type I <u>infs.</u>
have this, as does even one Type III
inf., a Minnesota stock-raiser. The variant <u>that the</u>, with but a single instance
in New England, appears 11 times in the
UM (though not at all in neighboring Wisconsin), also with majority use by Type I
infs.
   The theory that a compound sentence un-
derlies a sentence with a restrictive
relative is perhaps supported by the construction offered by 12 scattered infs.,

mostly in Type I. For them only a level
intonation contour unites in one sentence the elements <u>He's a boy</u> and <u>His
father is very rich</u> to form <u>He's a boy
his father is very rich</u>.
   Other devices to indicate the genitive
relationship between the two underlying
sentences appear in the following lexical and syntactic variants: "He's the
owner's boy"—52. ". . . the son of the
man that/who . . ."—59; 123-24, 134-36,
144-45. ". . . the son of the orchard
farmer"—128. ". . . the boy of the father
that . . ."—140; 421. ". . . that belongs
to the man that's got the orchard"—143.

	Type I	Type II	Type III
his	9%	5%	7%
that his	30%	11%	7%
that the	9%	5%	0
whose	49%	79%	87%

	Mn.	Ia.	N.D.	S.D.	Nb.	Ave.
his	9%	5%	4%	6%	9%	7%
that his	5%	30%	21%	31%	24%	19%
whose	70%	68%	67%	69%	56%	66%

POST-COPULA FORM

I/me

21.5 It wasn't <u>me</u>. NE 604.

Even in the somewhat less than casual
atmosphere of the interview situation the
majority of all UM infs. use <u>me</u>, not
school-taught <u>I</u>, in the preceding context.
   Except for a slightly lower frequency
of <u>I</u> in Nebraska no regional distribution
pattern appears. A social contrast is
evident, however, in the minimal occurrence of <u>I</u> among the least educated
speakers and its increased proportion
from one-fifth to nearly one-half on the
range between Type II and Type III.
   An additional contrast is found in the
fact that of the 24 infs. who use <u>I</u> in
this context 20, more than 80%, are wom-
en; and five of the 20 have taught in
grade school or high school.

	Type I	Type II	Type III
I	4%	20%	47%
me	96%	86%	60%

	Mn.	Ia.	N.D.	S.D.	Nb.	Ave.
I	17%	15%	13%	20%	8%	14%
me	88%	91%	96%	80%	80%	92%

I ?7, 18, 20, c22, 28, 33, 49, 58, 65; 102, 108, 110, 131, 152; 205, 214, 219; 312-13, 317, 319, 326; 406, 426, 431.

me 1-6, cr7, :8, 9-12, 14-15, 17, 19, 21-24, 26-27, *27, 29-30, c31, 32, 34-36, 38, 40-41, 48, 50, c54, 55-56, c57, 58, 62-64; 101, 104-9, 111-16, 118, c119, 121, 126, 128-29, 132-33, 135, 137-39, 143, cvr146, 148, 150, sn152; 201-4, sn205, 206-7, 209-18, 220-24, 226; 301-4, 308-11, ¹313, 314-16, 318, 320-25, 327-28; 401-5, 407-11, 413-25, 427-30, 432-33, sn434, 435-37.

no response 13, 16, 25, 37, 39, 42-47, 51-53, 59-61; 103, 117, 120, 122-25, 127, 130, 134, 136, 140-42, 144-45, 147, 149, 151; 208, 225; 305-7; 412.

Comment:
I: "'me' is wrong"—65. "Proper"—152. Inf. also said "This is she" in conversation—219. "I used to say 'me'"—312. me: "'Me' isn't proper, but I would say it except to someone like you"—22. Usu., "without thinking"—58. Inf. knows which he "ought to" use—108. Inf. knows 'I' is considered correct—128. Usu.—152. "But that's not correct"—226.

CHAPTER 5

Adjectivals

all

43.1 The oranges are <u>all</u> <u>gone</u>.

Intended to discover the possible extension of Pennsylvania <u>all</u>, this item is nonproductive. All informants in the UM have (<u>all</u>) <u>gone</u>.

poisonous

48.7 Some berries are <u>poisonous</u>. NE 251.

In predicative position two adjectivals occur, <u>poisonous</u> and <u>poison</u>. They are usually recorded in the context above, but occasionally in others, as in "A toadstool is poisonous."

In New England <u>poison</u> is general; <u>poisonous</u> is largely confined to the southern half, i.e., Massachusetts, Rhode Island, and Connecticut. For the UM a possible regional weighting appears in the slightly higher incidence of <u>poisonous</u> in the Northern speech territory. But a marked social pattern emerges from the field data. Although only one college graduate uses the simple <u>poison</u>, one-third of the Type II infs. and more than one-half of those in Type I have this form. <u>Poisonous</u>, conversely, is strongly favored by the more-educated speakers.

	Type I	Type II	Type III
poison	55%	32%	7%
poisonous	47%	67%	93%

	Mn.	Ia.	N.D.	S.D.	Nb.	Ave.
poison	36%	39%	31%	46%	57%	41%
poisonous	64%	61%	69%	54%	46%	59%

poison 4, 10, 15-16, *19, 22, 24-25, 29, 32, 35-36, 38-39, c40, 42, c46, 48, 54, 61-63, 65; 104-5, 107, c109, 111-12, 114, 118-19, 121, c132, 133, 135, 137-40, 142, 146-47; 204-5, 208-9, 214, 219-20, 224; c303, 306-7, 309, 311-12, c314, c317, 318, 320, 322-24; 401, 403, 405,

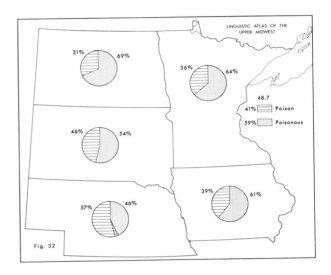

Fig. 32

408-10, 412, 414, cvr415, 416-17, 421, c422-23, 427, 429, c432, 433-34, c435, 436.

poisonous 1-3, 5-8, 11-14, 17-18, 20-21, 23, 26-28, 30-31, 33-34, 37, 41, c43-44, 45, 47, 49, c50-53, 55, 57-58, c59-60, 64; 101-2, c103, 106, 108, 110, c113, c115-16, 117, 120, 122-28, c129, 130-31, 134, 136, 141, 143-45, 148-50, 152; 201-3, 206-7, 210-13, 215-18, 221-23, 225-26; 301-2, 304, c305, 308, c310, c313, 315, c316, 319, 321, c325, 326-27, c328; 402, 404, 406-7, 411, c413, 418-20, 422, 424-26, 428, c430, 431, 437.

no response 9, 56; 151.

those

41.2 <u>those</u> boys. NE 625.

Two demonstrative adjectivals appear in this context to designate objects at some distance—<u>those</u> and <u>them</u>.

As in New England, the contrast between them in the UM seems social, not regional. None of the cultivated infs. and only one-fifth of the Type II infs. use them, but 60% of the least educated speakers use it. The redundant them there, fairly widespread in New England, is reported in the UM as found in the speech of only three Type I infs. in Minnesota and Iowa. The persistent attack of the schools upon this use of them is reflected in the fact that 17% of the infs. whose probable normal term is them shift to those in careful or guarded speech.

	Type I	Type II	Type III
them	60%	22%	0
those	61%	90%	100%

	Mn.	Ia.	N.D.	S.D.	Nb.	Ave.
them	40%	31%	40%	38%	53%	38%
those	74%	82%	72%	88%	65%	76%

them c4-6, cvr7, c8, c12-13, c15, cvr16, cvr19, c21-22, c25, c27, c31, c35, cvr41, c43, c48, c51-52, c56-57, c62;

c109, cvr112, c114, 118, c121, 132, 135, cvr138, 139-40, 142-43, 147; cvr203-4, c209, c211, cvr212, cvr216, c218, cvr220, c224, cvr225; c301, c303, 306-7, cvr311, ¹313, c314, cvr317, c321-22, *324; c401-4, cvr405, cvr407, c408, c415, cvr416, c417-18, cvr423, 424, c429-30, c432, c434, c436. them there c16; c109, c132.

those 1-2, c5-6, 9, c10-11, cvr13, 14, c15, 17-18, 20, c21-23, 24, 26, 28, c29, 30, 32, c33, 34, 36, 38-39, c40, c42, c44-47, c49, 50, c53, 54-57, c58-61, c63, 64-65; 101-8, 110-13, 115-31, 133-34, 136-38, 141, 144-46, 148-49; 201, c202-3, 205-8, cvr211, c213-14, 215, 217, 219, c221-22, 223, c224, 226; 301-5, 308-9, c310-11, 312-13, c314, 318-19, cvr320, c322, 323-26, c327, 328; c401, cvr403, c404, c408-10, 411, cvr413, 414, 416, c417, c419, 420-21, c422, 425, c426, 427-28, cvr431, 433, 435.

no response 3, 37; 150-52; 210, 315-16; 406, 412, 437.

CHAPTER 6

Articles

a(n)

41.1 Give me a(n) apple. NE 270.

Among UM infs. an is universal before a
vowel. Only two infs., Minnesota Type I
5 and 15, offer a [eˇ] [ə̆ˍ] before apple.

The customary pronunciation of an is
/ən/, but a more careful, perhaps stilt-
ed, form /æn/ appeared sometimes in the
interview situation. Of the various infs.
so recorded, one-half were reported by
fw. G. They are 20, 28, 32, 35, 39, 40,
45-48, 51, 53, 57-58, 60, 62-63; 103,
124, 130; 319; 416-18, 420, 426-27, 431.

the

15.1 I must wash (the) dishes. NE 137.

Wash dishes, as an idiom without the
definite article, is offered as a minor
variant, in contrast with wash the dishes, by a scattering of UM infs. There is
no marked regional or social contrast. Of

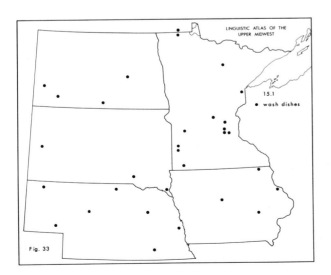

LINGUISTIC ATLAS OF THE
UPPER MIDWEST

15.1
● wash dishes

Fig. 33

the infs. who respond with wash instead
of do, the proportions of those with idi-
omatic wash dishes are as follows:

Mn.	Ia.	N.D.	S.D.	Nb.	Ave.
22%	11%	17%	14%	20%	17%

For the specific infs. see Volume 1.

the/(one's)

61.6 sick at the stomach. NE 503.

Although the primary significance of
this item lies in the choice of preposition (see section on prepositions), a
contrast also appears between frequency
of the definite article and that of the
possessive pronoun (his, my, etc.).

In New England a clear geographic distribution is manifest in the clustering
of responses with the in Vermont and in
Rhode Island and Connecticut. In the UM
regional contrast is less sharp, but social contrast is apparent.

Three of the five Canadian infs. have
the; otherwise its frequency does not
vary greatly as a minority form throughout the area, although there may be a
slight Midland orientation as is hinted
in the concentration in southern Iowa.
Ignoring the Canadian responses leads to
the following: Minnesota 9%, Iowa 15%,
North Dakota 15%, South Dakota 21%, and
Nebraska 11%, for an over-all average of
15%. All the other infs. have the possessive pronoun except the four not responding: 118, 151-52; 430.

The social contrast is marked by a 22%
frequency of the among Type I infs. and
only 8% among Type II infs. In addition,
three scattered Type III infs. use the
article rather than a pronoun. A very few
alternate between them.

the 1, 3, 13, 23, 46, 51, 59; 112, 122,
125-26, 135, 141, 145, 147, 149; 202,
204, c221, 223, 225; 306, 311, 314, 316,
324, 327; 403, 411, 420, 429.

CHAPTER 7

Conjunctions

65.7 I like him <u>because</u> he's so funny. NE 729.

The nearly universal joining form in the context above and similar ones is be-cause. In New England 15 widely scattered older and less-educated infs., 3%, use instead the phrase on <u>account of</u>. Malm-strom reports a similar frequency for this phrase in the Middle Atlantic states and a 6% frequency in the North Central region.

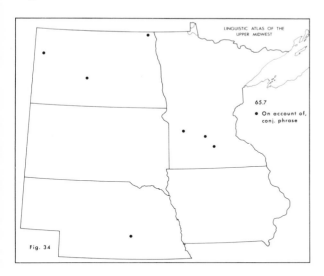

LINGUISTIC ATLAS OF THE UPPER MIDWEST

65.7

● On account of, conj. phrase

Fig. 34

In the UM about 3% of the infs. have <u>on account of</u>: 41, 44, c51; c207, c209, 216; cvr422. All are in the least educated group. Inf. 215 reports it as heard in his community. All other infs. have be-cause.

Through apheresis <u>because</u> often turns up as <u>'cause</u>. For this form and variant pronunciations see Volume 3.

65.5 It seems <u>like/as if</u> he'll never pull through. <u>NE 732.</u>

As an alternate to <u>as if</u> after <u>seems</u> or <u>looks</u> in this or a similar context, about one-sixth of the infs. in New England have <u>like</u>. Either a regional contrast or, as evidence suggests, a rapidly changing social status of <u>like</u> is indicated by its 74% frequency reported by Malmstrom for the North Central states and by its 56% frequency in the UM.

Although in New England <u>like</u> is rare among educated speakers, in the North Central states it is used by nearly one-half of the college graduates and by three-fourths of the high school gradu-ates. In the UM it is the choice of near-ly one-half of the college graduates and of more than one-half of the high school graduates.

Two phrasal conjunctions compete with <u>like</u>. More than one-third of the UM infs. use <u>as though</u> and one-sixth have <u>as if</u>, each of which is slightly favored by the more educated.

A scattering of UM infs., though none in Type III, have the minor variants <u>that</u>, <u>though</u>, <u>if</u>, <u>like as if</u>, and <u>likely</u>, and a few more get along with no conjunc-tion at all in this context.

It may be observed that this construc-tion, though also a point at issue in the schools, is not the same as that in which usage contrast is between <u>like</u> and simple <u>as</u>, e.g., "Our representative always votes <u>like/as</u> we want him to."

	Type I	Type II	Type III
as if	12%	13%	38%
as though	26%	24%	31%
like	56%	56%	44%
that	5%	5%	0
though	5%	5%	0

	Mn.	Ia.	N.D.	S.D.	Nb.	Ave.
as if	18%	8%	27%	13%	11%	15%
as though	23%	26%	38%	13%	29%	26%
like	56%	52%	46%	74%	54%	56%
that	7%	0	0	9%	9%	5%
though	0	14%	0	4%	0	4%

as if [1]1, c13, c15, 18, c19-20, 28-29, 34, c55, c59; 109, 126, 131, 134; 205, 208, 210, 212, c215, 218, 226; 319, 321, 326; 415, c419, 426, s435, 437.

as though 2-3, 10-12, 22, 27, ?28, 38, 42, 50, c54, sn56, 61, f62; 103, c107, 108, 112, 121, *123, 129-30, 132-33, sn143, 144, 148, s150; 201-2, 204, 207, c208, 219, 221-23, 225; cvr308, 314, 326; 409, :410, c413, 420, c422, 424, 428, 432-33, 436.

if 48; 116, 139; 423.

like [1]1, c4, 5, c6, 7-9, c14-17, c19, sn21, c24-25, 26, c30-31, 32, 34, c35, 37, 39, c40, 41, c44, s48, 49, c51, 58-60, c63, sn64; 102, 104-7, 110, s[1]111, 114-15, 117, 122-25, 127-28, 136, 140-42, 145-47, 149, c150, c152; c203, sn206, c209, c211, c213, 214, c215, 216, c217, 220, 223, c224; c301, 303-4, 306-7, 309-11, c312, 313, 315, c316, 320, 322, c324-25, 328; c401, 402, c403-6, 408, 411, c412-13, 416, c417-18, 421, cvr423, 425, c427, c429, 433.

like as if 60. likely 21, 33.

that 21, c23, 32, 36, f62; 309-10; sn414, 428, 435.

though 101, 113, 119-20, c133, 135, 138; 323.

no subordinating conjunction 1, 28, 65; 137; 414, 431, 434.

no response 43, 45-48, 52-53, 57; 118, 151; 302, 305, 317-18, 327; 407, 430.

unless

65.6 I won't go unless he goes. NE 730.

At the time of the New England survey without strongly competed with unless in

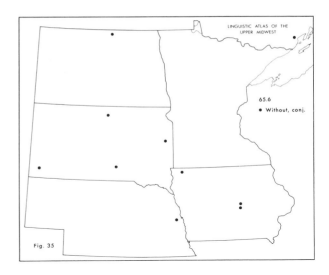

Fig. 35

the preceding context. Nearly one-half of all infs. are shown in *The Linguistic Atlas of New England* to have without, its incidence being highest in eastern Massachusetts, New Hampshire, and Maine. According to Malmstrom without is somewhat competitive in the Middle Atlantic states as well, with one-fifth of the infs. using it; in the North Central states the proportion drops to one-seventh of the infs., most of whom are Type I's.

In the UM the status of without corresponds with that in the North Central region. Only 10 widely scattered speakers, all but one in Type I, offer it: 3; c101, 132-33; c204; c303, c317, c320, 321; 427.

All other infs. have unless except two, one of whom, inf. 316, has simple less, and the other of whom, inf. 417, has except, not found in *The Linguistic Atlas of New England*, in ". . . not except Ralph does."

CHAPTER 8

Prepositions

after

26.2 We named the child <u>after</u> him. NE 394.

In the UM two prepositions, <u>after</u> and <u>for</u>, occur in this or a similar context, <u>as</u> with <u>father</u> or <u>grandfather</u> instead of the <u>pronoun</u>.

Although <u>after</u> predominates in New England, <u>for</u> is also quite common, chiefly in Maine and eastern Massachusetts, sections that have had little influence upon speech west of the Berkshires. UM speakers in all groups so strongly prefer <u>after</u> that here <u>for</u> is clearly a receding <u>form</u>. Except for a few instances in the western Dakotas, its distribution is limited to the first settled portions of the UM.

	Type I	Type II	Type III
after	93%	89%	100%
for	9%	17%	6%

	Mn.	Ia.	N.D.	S.D.	Nb.	Ave.
after	95%	88%	92%	78%	95%	92%
for	11%	15%	8%	22%	6%	12%

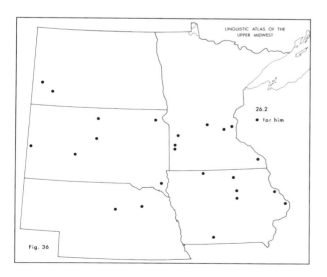

LINGUISTIC ATLAS OF THE UPPER MIDWEST

26.2
• for him

Fig. 36

after 1-29, 31-35, c36, 37-41, 43, c44, 45, c46, 48-65; 101-2, 104-5, s107, 108-17, 119, *120, 121-22, *123, 124-38, 140-43, 145-52; 201-13, 216, :217, 218-26; 301-3, 305-6, 308-9, ¹310, 311-12, :313, 314, 316-23, 325-28; 401-8, 410-13, 416-37.

for ¹10, 30, 37, *39, 42, 46-47, ?54, 58; 103, 106, 116, 118, 120, 123, 139, 144; 214-15; 304, c308, 310, ¹312, 313, 315, 324; 414-15.

no response 307; 409.

Comment:
<u>after</u>: "I think that is better than 'for'"—10.

at (once)

2.6 Everything seemed to happen all <u>at once</u>.

Although <u>all to once</u> occurs sporadically as a minor <u>variant</u> in New York State and northern Pennsylvania, its meager popularity decreased even more with the westward movement. In the UM only four Type I speakers have it—two in Minnesota and two in South Dakota. The nearly universal phrase is <u>all at once</u>. Four equivalent expressions occur once each.

This and the two following phrases with <u>at</u>, <u>at home</u> and <u>at the stomach</u>, are dealt with in Virginia McDavid, "<u>To</u> as a preposition of location in Linguistic Atlas Materials," *Publication of the American Dialect Society* 40(1963), 12-19.

all at once 1-12, c13, 14-40, 42, ?43, 44, f45, !46, 47-58, c59, 60, 62-65; 101-17, 119-39, 141-49, sf150, 152; 201-5, 207-26; 301-10, 312-13, 315-26, c327; 401-6, c407, 408-23, c424, 425-33, 435-37.

all at the same time c60. all of a sudden 21. all together 140. all to once 41, cvr59; 311, 314. in a bunch 57.

no response 61; 118, 151; 206; 328; 434.

at (home)

25.6 There's nobody <u>at</u> home. NE 403.

Two prepositional phrases with <u>at</u> or <u>to</u> and the simple locative adverb <u>home</u> are found in the context above.

Malmstrom's data from the eastern dialect projects reveal the dominant status of <u>at</u> in all areas and, except in New England, among all infs. There <u>to</u> occurs among all groups and is the most frequent term among the older and more old-fashioned speakers. <u>To</u> also occurs in New York and northern Pennsylvania and in the Northern speech area of the North Central states (38% in Wisconsin, 30% in Michigan, 15% in Ohio, but none in Kentucky). The simple adverb <u>home</u> is a widespread minority form among all speakers, with a general average of 14% in New England and 21% in the North Central states.

Although <u>at</u> home likewise has over-all dominance in the UM, the most common form in North Dakota is simple <u>home</u>. Home generally is proportionately more frequent than in the eastern investigations and apparently is expanding at the expense of <u>to</u> home, which is clearly recessive, with

	Mn.	Ia.	N.D.	S.D.	Nb.	Ave.
home	35%	35%	58%	25%	11%	33%
at home	74%	63%	42%	64%	95%	70%
to home	3%	13%	12%	14%	5%	9%

at home 1-3, 9-13, c14, c16, 17, 20, 22, 24, c25, 27-34, 36-38, 40-43, 45-49, 51-53, 55-58, c59-60, 61-63, 65; 102-4, 106, 110-12, 116, 118-19, *120, 122-23, 125-28, 130, 133-35, 137-39, 142-44, 146-47, 149-52; 207, c208, 211, 215, 218-19, c220, 221-22, 224, 226; 301-3, 305, 309-10, 312-17, c322, 324-28; 401-4, 406-27, r428, 429-33, s434, 435-37.

home 4-5, c6, 7-8, c13, c15, 16-19, 21, 23, 25-26, 31, 34-35, 38, 50, 54, 63-64; 101, 105, 107-8, 113-15, 120-22, 124, 129, 131, 136, 140-41, 145, 148; 201-6, 209-10, 212-15, 217, 220, 223; 304, *306, 307, c317, 318, c319, 323, 325, 328; 426, 430-31, 434.

to home c39, s†40, c44, ¹60; c104-5, c108-9, 117, 132, c139; c203, c216, c225; 311, 320-21, c327; 405, 421, ¹435.

Comment:
<u>at</u> home: "I suppose more properly one should say 'at home'"—34. <u>to</u> home: Heard from older people—435.

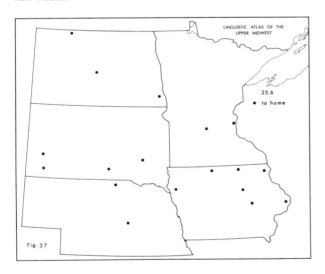

LINGUISTIC ATLAS OF THE UPPER MIDWEST

25.6
• to home

Fig. 37

no Type III instances and with twice as many among the oldest and least educated as among the high school graduates. Fws. also recorded some stray instances of to = at during the interviews: "a funeral I was to"—104; "I was to a picnic"—139; "They was down to Lincoln"—416; "We was out to California"—436.

	Type I	Type II	Type III
home	33%	30%	50%
at home	63%	76%	75%
to home	12%	7%	0

at (the stomach)

61.1 sick <u>at</u> the stomach. NE 509. WG 14, 78; F152.

Both regional and social contrasts appear in the choice of preposition in the specific context above.

Kurath finds <u>to</u> the <u>stomach</u> dominating most of New England and its western settlement area in New York State, with <u>at</u> your stomach not only common in the Midland region but also used by younger and more cultured speakers in metropolitan New York and southwestern New England, presumably as an expanding form. <u>In your</u> stomach turns up in the Philadelphia trade area, and <u>on your stomach</u> is characteristic of Pennsylvania German speakers. In the North Central States <u>to</u> continues to be obviously a Northern choice, as Virginia McDavid points out.

Data in the UM rather clearly point to the continuing western extension of <u>to</u>, despite textbook objections, rather than of <u>at</u>, which is a feeble minor variant in Minnesota and the Dakotas and even in Midland Iowa and Nebraska barely scrapes up a 50% frequency—and that only because of its higher proportion among the less-educated infs. <u>To</u> not only dominates Minnesota and the Dakotas and is quite strong in Iowa and Nebraska but also is

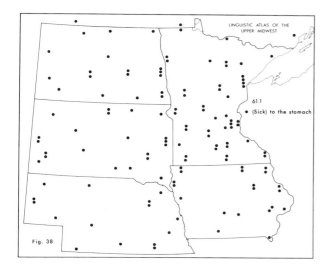

Fig. 38

especially favored by the most highly
educated.

Consistently, Pennsylvania *in the stomach* survives chiefly in southern Iowa,
and still rarer Pennsylvania *on the stomach* is used by only three Midland speakers, two in Iowa and one in Nebraska.

Three prepositions not reported in the
East turn up in the UM. Two instances of
highly graphic *from his stomach* are in
the Dakotas, one of *sympathetic with his
stomach* in Minnesota, and one of *possibly
ambiguous of his stomach* in Iowa.

	Type I	Type II	Type III
at	32%	26%	13%
in	13%	3%	0
to	52%	68%	94%

	Mn.	Ia.	N.D.	S.D.	Nb.	Ave.
at	14%	47%	12%	11%	53%	28%
in	8%	16%	4%	4%	3%	8%
to	77%	41%	77%	79%	42%	62%

at 2, 13, 29, 33, 48, 51, 54, 56, 59;
cr103, 111-12, c113, 115, 120, 123, 125,
127-28, 130-31, 133, 135, 137, 139, 141-
42, 145-49; 208, 212-13; 311, 314, 324;
401, 403, c405, 406, 411-14, 418, 420-21,
c422, 423-24, 427, 429, 434-36.
  from 209; 323.
  in 7, 19, 35, 44, 46; 104, 114, 124,
126, 129, 132, 136, 145; 202; 306.
  of 149.
  on 143, 145; 307.
  to 1, 3-5, c6, 8-12, 14-18, *19, 20-23,
25-28, 30-31, f32, 34, 36-38, c39, 40-43,
ᴸ44, 45, 47, ᴸ48, 49-50, 52-53, 55, 57-
58, 60-65; 101-2, ?103, 105-10, 116,
c117, 119, 121-23, *131, 134, 137-38,
140, 144, 150; 201, 203-5, 207, 210-11,
214-20, c221, 222-26; 301-4, c305, 308-
10, 312-13, 315-22, 325-28; 402, 404,

408-10, 415-17, 419, s425, 426, 431-33,
437.
  with 24.
  no response 118, 151-52; 430.

Comment:
  in: Inf. insists he uses this and has
heard it often--7.

behind

9.3 The broom is behind the door. NE
723.

In the pre-broom closet era an open
kitchen door often concealed the broom.
To describe its relation to the door, or
any similar relationship, behind or (in)
back of is customarily used.
  Behind predominates in all groups by a
4:1 or 3:1 ratio in the New England and
Middle Atlantic states; in the North Central region the incidence of back of increases to more than one-third, but with
no significant variation among the three
groups. In back of, a variant often cas-
tigated in textbooks despite its obvious
analogy with accepted in front of, is a
minority variant throughout the East.

In the UM behind and back of maintain a
2:1 ratio, with in back of having a general 7% incidence because of its higher
frequency in Minnesota and North Dakota
than in Iowa and Nebraska. This distribution contrasts with that in the North
Central states, where in back of is more
frequent in the Midland speech section.
Aside from this variation in the UM, however, no marked regional or social pattern emerges.

	Type I	Type II	Type III
back of	26%	27%	31%
in back of	8%	7%	0
behind	71%	73%	75%

	Mn.	Ia.	N.D.	S.D.	Nb.	Ave.
back of	20%	37%	31%	32%	19%	27%
in back of	14%	2%	8%	4%	3%	7%
behind	71%	65%	62%	80%	84%	72%

back of 4, 13, c15, 16, 19, 21, 23, 26,
47-48, 51, !52, 61, 63-64; 101-2, 104-5,
c111, 112, 118, 123, 130, 132, 136, 138-
40, 143, 148-50; 201, 203, 209, 214, 216-
17, 221, 224; c302, 307-8, ?309, 316,
319, :!323, 326, 328; 406, 413, 419-22,
c426. in back of 24, 30, 42, c45, *48,
49, c52, 55, 62; 141; 219, 225; 305;
c408.
  behind 1, !2, 3, 5-12, c13-14, 15, 17-
18, 20, 22, 25, 27-29, 31-40, *41, 43-44,
c!46, 47, 50, c53, 54, 56-58, c59, 60,
65; 103, 106-11, 113-17, 119-20, c121,
122, 124-25, 127, 129, *130, 131, 133-35,

137, 142, 144, 146-47, 151-52; 202, 204-8, 210-13, 215, 218, c220, 222, !223, 226; 301-5, *306, cr309, 310-11, 313-14, 316-18, 320, !321, 324, 326-27; 401-2, !403-4, 405, !407, 408-12, 414-18, 420-21, 423-25, 427-29, c430, 431-37. in behind 322.
   on the other side 17.
   no response 126, 128, 145; 312, 315, 325.

Comment:
   back of: "More common"—326. behind: "'Behind the door' would be better"—309.

(wait) for

72.3 I'll wait for you.

   After wait only four UM infs., all in Midland speech territory, have the preposition on: 143, 150; c417, 434. All others have for. There are no responses from 118 and 151.

in

19.5 Burn coal in the stove.

   A suspected contrast between in and into in this context did not turn up in the UM. Only two infs. have into, both using it in free conversation: 7 and 10. Inf. 40 terms it "old-fashioned," and inf. 25 reports having heard it from others. Other infs. use in.

(died) of

59.5 I don't know what he died of. NE 519.

   Three prepositions, from, of, and with, are widely found as possible after die in the context above (or as in "He died of tuberculosis"). Of is dominant in New England and barely so in the UM. The relative strength of the two other terms, however, is not the same in the UM as in the East. With, offered by nearly 40% of the infs. throughout New England and by more than one-fourth of those in the North Central state of Wisconsin, survives in the UM with only an 18% frequency among Type I and Type II speakers that suggests a Midland orientation because of the weighting in Iowa and Nebraska. It is not found in Type III. On the other hand, from, which has a scanty 4.5% frequency in New England, has approximately a 25% frequency in Wisconsin and in the UM is used by one-third of the infs. in the

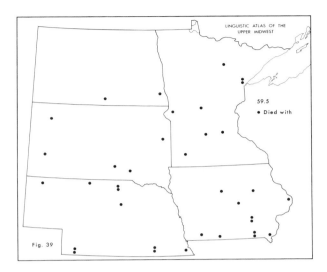

Fig. 39

three groups, and with a possible slight Northern orientation.
   A solitary use of died on by a Russo-German in North Dakota is surely derived from German *sterben an.*

	Type I	Type II	Type III
die from	31%	33%	44%
die of	45%	59%	63%
die with	29%	8%	0

	Mn.	Ia.	N.D.	S.D.	Nb.	Ave.
die from	40%	30%	35%	25%	29%	33%
die of	52%	54%	54%	54%	46%	52%
die with	12%	22%	8%	18%	29%	18%

   from c1, 4-5, 8, 10, 12, 17-19, 23-24, 26, cr28, 31, 34, c36, 37, 39, †40, 41, 43, :¹44, 47, 50, 52, 55, 60, 62, ¹63; 106, 108-13, 115, 131, 138, 140, 143-44, 149-50; 203-6, c209, 210, 212, 216, 221; 302-3, 305-7, s308, ¹309, 318, 328; 404, 407-8, 414, 417, 421, 423, 427, 435-36.
   of 2-3, 6-7, 9, ¹10, c13, 14-16, 20, c21, 22, :?28, 29-30, :?32, 33, 38, 40, c42, 44-46, ¹47, 48-49, 51, 53-54, 56-58, 61-65; 101-5, 107, 110, 116, 118-30, 133-34, 137, 141, 145, 149; 201-2, 207-8, 211, 213-15, 217-20, 222, 226; 304, 309-10, 312-16, 319-20, 323-27; 402, 409-12, 416-20, 422, 424-26, 428, 431.
   on 224.
   with 11, c15-16, 25, 27, c35, 44, 59; 114, 117, s118, ¹124, 132, 135-36, 139, 142, *145, 146-48; 223, 225; 301, 311, 317, 321, c322; 401, 403, 405-6, 413, 429, 432-34, 437.
   no response 151-52; 415, 430.

Comment:
   died from: Used by inf.'s mother—40. Inf. says a sentence should not end with a preposition—47. "I suppose we should say 'died of'"—55. "More formal" than

66

'died of'—55. died with: Inf. says this is not "proper"—124.

(quarter) of (eleven)

4.7 quarter of eleven. NE 81.

In the UM the more common designation of a specific time before the even hour is with to as in a quarter to eleven. More than one-half of the informants have to; one-third use competing of. Each manifests a regional pattern, to being stronger in Northern speech territory and of in Midland. This situation correlates with that in New England, where, although of predominates and to is a minority form, to is proportionately stronger in the Southwest, the region that has particularly provided the base for Northern speech.

Midland till, unrecorded in New England, is found in southern Iowa and, sparsely, in Nebraska and South Dakota.

A few scattered infs. insist that instead of quarter they regularly or occasionally use fifteen minutes.

The modern technical expression, e.g., ten forty-five, is found throughout the UM, especially among younger infs., but the data are incomplete because fws. Wr and P did not record it.

	Type I	Type II	Type III
of	31%	34%	19%
till	7%	9%	6%
to	52%	49%	56%

	Mn.	Ia.	N.D.	S.D.	Nb.	Ave.
of	28%	44%	15%	18%	40%	31%
till	2%	22%	0	7%	8%	8%
to	63%	34%	77%	71%	46%	51%

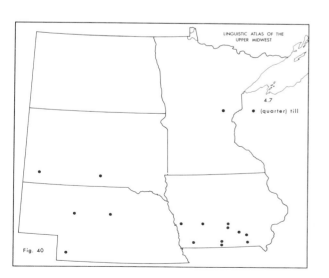

LINGUISTIC ATLAS OF THE UPPER MIDWEST

4.7 (quarter) till

Fig. 40

fifteen (minutes) of (to) 24; 146; 209-10; 305, 307, 316, 322-23; 417, 430.

quarter of 11-12, ¹20, 21, 28, c29, 30, 33, 37, cr39, 43, 47, 52-53, 55, 59-60, 62, 65; 101, 104, 106-7, ¹111, 113, 116, 120-23, 126, 128, 130, 133, 138, 141, 143, 146-49; 152; 210, 214, 222-23; 307, c313, 318, 324, †326, 328; 401, cr403, 406, 417, 420, 422, c424, 426-28, 431-32, c433, 436-37.

quarter till 23; 124, 127, 129, 131, 134, 136, 142, 144-46, 149; ¹310, 320-21; 412, 414, 429.

quarter to 2-3, 5-8, ¹*9, 10, 13-19, 22, 24-27, 31-32, 34, †35, 36, 39-42, 44-46, 48-51, 54, 56, cr57, 58, *62, 63-64; 102, 105, 108-10, 112, 114-15, 117, 125, 127, 132, 135, 137, 139-40, 150; 201-3, c204, 205-9, 211-12, ¹213, 215-21, ¹223, 224, ¹225, 226; 301-6, 309-17, 319, 322-23, 325, 327; 403, ¹404, 405, 407-11, 413, 415-16, 418-19, 421, 425, 430, 434-35.

ten forty-five 1, 4, 9-10, 17, 20-22, c24, 28, 34-35, 38, 58; 101, 103, 106, 111, 119-20; 205, 207, 210, 213, 216, →217, 218-19, 225; 308, ¹309, 312, 319, 326; 402, 404-5, 410, 423, 433. ten and three-quarters 15.

no response 61; 118, 151.

Comment:

quarter to: Casual—10. Occas.—24, 34; 207. Rare—219. -forty-five: To indicate specific appointment—10. Exactness probably due to husband's influence—20. Occas.—22. Usu.—34; 219. As a railroad man he always says this—119. Usu., as his work is with railroad people—207. "Radio influence"—217. fifteen minutes: Occas.—24. "I wouldn't say 'quarter'"—209.

off

28.1a He fell off the horse. NE 724.

In the foregoing and similar contexts Malmstrom finds the widespread majority form to be off among all groups from New England and the Middle Atlantic states to the North Central region, with the proportion higher in the Middle Atlantic area (nearly nine-tenths) than elsewhere (about two-thirds). The proportion is also higher among the better educated informants (100% in New England, 98% in the Middle Atlantic states, 84% in the North Central states).

In New England the chief competitor is off'n, used by more than one-fourth of the less educated; but elsewhere it is the compound off of, which is very strong in the Middle Atlantic region and which, despite school and dictionary disparage-

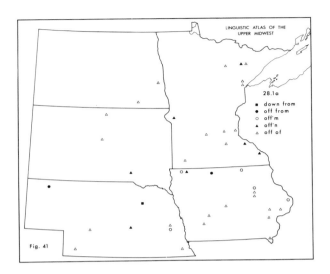

Fig. 41

LINGUISTIC ATLAS OF THE
UPPER MIDWEST

28.1a
● down from
● off from
○ off'm
▲ off'n
△ off of

102, 104, 106-11, 113-15, 117, 119-22,
c123, 125-26, 129-36, 138-39, 141, 143,
145-49; 201-23, 226; 301-2, 304-5, 307-
10, 312-18, 320-21, c323, 324-26, 328;
401-9, c410, 411-14, 416-18, 420-23,
s425, 426-28, 430-33, 435-37.
    off'm c101, c105, c116, c139; c424.
    off'n c13, r26, c55-56; cvr101; 322;
c421.
    off from 103; 402.
    off of 11, c13, c15-16, 34, 40, 43, 48,
60; 117-18, 127-28, 137, 140, 150-52;
c222, 224; 303, c314; 419, 424, 429, 434.
    no response 311, 327.

Comment:
    off: "The correct expression"—58.

on

22.8   The coat has buttons on it.

    A suggested regional contrast between
on and onto in this context barely exists
in the UM. Two Minnesota infs., 10 and
16, were heard using onto in free conversation; one other, 48, acknowledged using
it. Other infs. use on.

past

4.6   half past seven.   NE 80.

    In the UM the preposition joining half
to the hour term is almost unanimously
past. An older variant, after, common in
northeastern New England but even there
often characterized as old-fashioned,
survives in the UM with only one inf., a
Duluth, Minnesota, Type I of English parentage. Two Minnesota auxiliary infs. report having heard it in their communities, one terming it a "smart-alecky
Yankee expression."
    But half past is itself declining in
face of competition from the newer compound with -thirty following the hour
term, as seven-thirty, a mode consistent
with such phrases as seven-fourteen
(7:14) and seven thirty-four (7:34) de-
manded in numerous aspects of contemporary technological society.
    Only a deceptive regional contrast ap-
pears in the UM. The higher proportion of
seven-thirty in Nebraska correlates with
the data from the field records of fw.
Wr, who apparently accepted this as a
first response without seeking an alternate; the lower proportion in Iowa coin-
cides with the data from the field records of fw. P, who apparently disregarded
seven-thirty as a response.
    Other fws. found so high a proportion

ment, in the North Central states is used
by 50% of the Type I speakers, 35% of the
Type II's, and 25% of the Type III's.
Off'n is the choice of one-fifth of the
Types I and II infs. in the North Central
region. Simple from, frequent in northern
New England, is rare elsewhere; the
phrasal off from has similar status except that it is slightly more frequent in
southwestern New England and is frequent
in the North Central state of Wisconsin.
    In the UM off is likewise the dominant
form, slightly favored by the better educated. Off of is the minority term found
in all three groups, most frequent in
Type I and perhaps here with Midland orientation. Off'n and off'm are clearly of
nonstandard occurrence and perhaps also
have Midland bias. The full phrase off
from comes from only two Midland speakers. None of the phrasal expressions are
used by the Canadian infs., and they are
rare in the western fringe of the UM.

	Type I	Type II	Type III
from	9%	7%	25%
off	69%	90%	81%
off'm/off'n	8%	4%	0
off of	17%	7%	19%

	Mn.	Ia.	N.D.	S.D.	Nb.	Ave.
from	12%	13%	4%	4%	5%	9%
off	75%	69%	92%	77%	84%	78%
off'm/off'n	6%	8%	0	4%	5%	5%
off of	14%	17%	8%	8%	11%	13%

    down from 415.
    from 3, 7, 36, 45-46, 52, 58, 63; 112,
130-31, 142, 144, 150, 152; 225; 319;
404, 425.
    off 1-2, 4-6, 8-10, 12, c13-14, c16-18,
19-25, 27-33, 35, 37-39, 41-42, 44-45,
47, 49-51, 53-54, 57-59, 61-62, 64-65;

of infs. who use both forms that a total of more than one-fourth of all infs. are so recorded. What determines the choice of seven-thirty or half past seven at a given moment is not apparent within the limits of this investigation.

	Type I	Type II	Type III
half past	76%	67%	62%
-thirty	51%	58%	62%

	Mn.	Ia.	N.D.	S.D.	Nb.	Ave.
half past	78%	76%	73%	71%	51%	71%
-thirty	58%	38%	78%	46%	62%	55%

half after seven 15, *¹46, *¹62.

half past seven 2-3, ¹5, 6-8, ?10, 11-14, 16-19, ¹20, 22-23, c25, 26, c29, 30, c31, 32-34, c35, 36, †38, 39-43, r44, 45-48, 50-56, c57, 58, c59, 60, 62-65; 102, 105, 107, 109-10, 113, 115-17, 120, 122-32, 134-36, 138-50, 152; 201-2, †203, 205-6, c207, 208-12, ¹213, 214-18, 220, 223-24, ¹225, 226; 301-2, 305-7, c309, 310-11, †312, 313-20, ¹321, 322-23, †324-26, 327-28; c401, †402, 403, ¹404, 405-7, †409, 410, 412, ¹413, 414-15, 417-20, c424, 426, 429, 431, 436-37.

seven thirty 1, 4-5, 7-9, cr10, 11-12, 14-15, 17, 19-24, 26-28, 30, 32-35, c36, 37, c38, 39, 41, c42, 49, 55, 58, 63-64; 101-4, 106, 108, 111-14, 116-17, 119-21, 133, 137, 148, 150; →203, c204, 205-8, →209, 211-13, 215, →216, 217-19, 221-22, 224-26; 303-6, 308, →312, 314, 319, 321, 323-25, →326; 402-4, 408-10, c411, 413, 416-17, 420-22, cvr423, 425, 427-28, →429, 430, c432, 433-35.

no response 61; 118, 151.

Comment:
half after: "a smart-alecky Yankee expression"—62. half past: Occas.—7; 207; 324. Usu.—8, 22, 36; 215, 217; 403. Common—12. Old expression—14, 42. Heard seldom—20. Thinks he used to say this all the time—23. Used as a boy—38. "Rare" in community—64. Infrequent—226. seven-thirty: Would say '19:30' for p.m.—1. Usu.—10, 34, 42, 49, 64; 150; 205-7, 219, 226; 323, 324; 410. Occas.—22. Local ex-

pression—28. More exact—33. "Shorter"—34. Says railroads have changed people's way of telling time—225. More likely—319.

toward

25.8 He came toward me. NE 722.

In such a context as this, two variants widely occur. Towards, usual in British English and common in Canada, is usually listed in American dictionaries simply as a variant with no indication of the usage contrast found both in New England and in the UM.

Since the item was added to the worksheets near the completion of the Minnesota fieldwork, data from that state are fragmentary, but the returns elsewhere in the UM show that, as in New England, towards is favored by the less educated and toward by the more highly educated. No college graduate in the UM offers towards.

There seem to be no marked regional contrasts.

	Type I	Type II	Type III
toward	40%	54%	100%
towards	63%	48%	0

	Ia.	N.D.	S.D.	Nb.	Ave.
toward	46%	46%	50%	59%	49%
towards	56%	54%	54%	46%	52%

toward 38; 101, 103, 105, 107, 110-11, c115, 116-18, 121-22, 125-29, 131-33, 135, 145, 149-50; 203, c208, 210-14, 217-18, 220, c221, 222; *306, 309-13, c315, 316, 318-19, 324-26; 401-4, 406, 410-12, c414, 419, 421, c422, 423-27, 431-33, 435-36.

towards c13, 16, c29-31, c35-36; 102, 104, 106, 108-9, 112-15, 119-20, 123-24, 130, 134, 136-44, 146-48, 151-52; c201, 202, 204-7, 209, 215-16, 219, c223, 224-26; 301-4, 307, c314, 316-17, cvr320, 321-22, c323, c327-28; c403, 405, cvr407, 408, c409, c413, 415-18, 420, 428-30, sn434, 437.

CHAPTER 9

Adverbs

anywhere

33.3 You can find that anywhere around here. NE 709.

In this context infs. in the eastern and North Central dialect studies respond with anywhere, anywheres, and anyplace. No marked regional pattern has been found, as the same broad proportions appear throughout, with anywhere most common but with anywheres showing Northern orientation in the North Central states. A social variation appears in the lower frequency of anyplace and anywheres among educated speakers, to the extent that no Type III infs. offer anyplace in and around the New York and Washington, D.C., metropolitan areas.

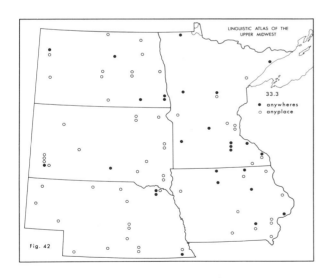

Fig. 42

LINGUISTIC ATLAS OF THE
UPPER MIDWEST

33.3
● anywheres
○ anyplace

In the UM standard anywhere likewise dominates anywheres, which, though offered by two college graduates, clearly is more strongly favored by the less educated. A regional contrast appears in the distribution of anyplace, which is

much stronger in the three western states than in Minnesota and Iowa, and possibly in the distribution of anywheres, which has a slight Northern orientation.

	Type I	Type II	Type III
anyplace	33%	32%	13%
anywhere	55%	80%	80%
anywheres	18%	8%	12%

	Mn.	Ia.	N.D.	S.D.	Nb.	Ave.
anyplace	13%	22%	42%	62%	46%	31%
anywhere	77%	84%	50%	42%	82%	66%
anywheres	17%	12%	19%	8%	8%	13%

anyplace c16, 22, 26, 31, 36-37, 57, 65; 106-7, 109, 121, 129, 136-37, 144, 148, 150, 152; 204, 206, 210, 213-14, 216-20, 223; 302, 305-7, 311-13, 317-18, 320, 323-26, 328; 401, 404-5, 407, 409, 414-15, 417, 420-22, 431-35, 437.
anywhere 1-5, 7-12, c13, 14-15, 17-18, 20, 22-29, 32-34, 38-42, 44-47, c49, 51-54, 57-63, 65; 101-3, 105-8, 110-12, 114-15, 117-34, 136-39, 141-50, 152; c201, 202-3, 205, 208, 210-13, 215, f216, 221, sn223; 301-2, cr304, 308, 310, 314-15, 322, 326, :328; 402-4, 406, 410-13, cvr414, 416, 418-19, 421, 423, s424, 425, 427-30, 432, sn433, s434, c436.
anywheres 4, c6, c19, c21, c43, c46, 48-50, 55-56; c104-5, 113, 116, 135, 140; 209, c211, 224, c225, 226; ?304, c320, 321; c407, 408, 426, s435.

as far as

In the index of Volume 1 there is a cross-reference to this volume for the expressions all the farther, as far as, and farthest. The reference is an error, since a later decision led to the inclusion of these items in the first volume.

a-purpose

75.3 He did it a-purpose. NE 719.

Intention in this context is usually

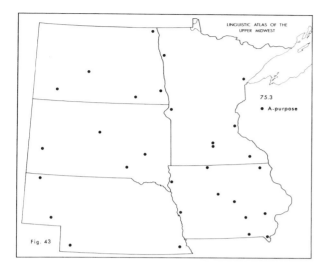

LINGUISTIC ATLAS OF THE
UPPER MIDWEST

75.3
• A-purpose

Fig. 43

shown by an adverbial expression with
purpose.
In New England both a-purpose and on
purpose are common, with the former
strongest in northern New England and the
latter in the southwestern sector. Purposely is a minor variant.
In the UM on purpose is by far the majority form, with no marked geographical
variation. A-purpose, aphetized to simple
purpose by inf. 13, survives but with
sharply declining vigor. No college graduates use it, and only a few Type II
infs. in Minnesota and Iowa. Its remaining strength appears chiefly among the
least educated speakers.

	Type I	Type II	Type III
a-purpose	23%	8%	0
on purpose	74%	89%	94%
purposely	9%	9%	13%

	Mn.	Ia.	N.D.	S.D.	Nb.	Ave.
a-purpose	9%	20%	19%	17%	11%	15%
on purpose	88%	80%	73%	74%	89%	82%
purposely	11%	6%	15%	22%	0	9%

deliberate 14; 435.
intentional 13. intentionally 18, 20,
34; 307; 432-33.
purposely 14, 17, 19-20, 23, 36, 58;
101-2, 106; 214, 217, 219, 222; 311,
→312, 316-17, c324.
a-purpose 8, 13, 15, 25, 40, ¹48, c51,
52, ¹58, 64; c103, c107, c109, 115, 124,
c132, 135, c138, 147, 149; 207, 215-16,
224-25; sn311, †312, c314, 322, 327; 401,
417, 429, 434.
on purpose 1-7, 9-13, 16-18, sn19, s20,
21-24, 26-31, c32, 33-35, sn36, 37-50,
cr?51, 53-57, ¹58, c59, 60-65; 101, 104-
6, 108, 110-14, 116-17, c119-20, 121-23,
125-31, 133-34, 136-46, 148, 150, 152;

201-6, 208-13, ¹217, 218, sn219, :220,
221-23, 226; 301-5, *306, 309-10, 313,
315, 318-21, 323, :325, †326, 328; 402-6,
:407, 408-9, c410, 411-12, sn413, 414-16,
418-28, 430-31, sn432-33, 435-37.
no response 118, 151; 308.

Comment:
a-purpose: "Writing, we would put 'on'
in there"—149. on purpose: "More likely
to say this"—64. "Children say this"—217.

(want) off, (want) in

64.2   I want to get off at the next cor-
ner. NE 699. WG 30, 79; F15, F159.

In the statement above, made to a
streetcar conductor or bus operator, most
infs. in the investigated areas use the
full expression want to get off. More
than four out of five UM infs. have this.
But a significant proportion of UM
speakers, one-fifth, offer a simple variant want off, with the meaning of the
verb of motion borne entirely by off.
Want off appears only once in *The Linguistic Atlas of New England*, in the conversation of a New Brunswick inf. of
Scotch and northern Irish ancestry, but
it is common in Pennsylvania—except in
the northern and northeastern sectors,
and it is common also in western Virginia
and West Virginia.
The strength of want off in Pennsylvania and the existence of an analogous
construction in German led some earlier
students of American English to infer a
direct influence of Pennsylvania German.
Albert H. Marckwardt, however, adducing
early nineteenth-century Scottish quota-
tions in the *Oxford English Dictionary*,
finds the likely source to be the speech
of the Scotch-Irish in Pennsylvania, a
finding consistent with the frequency of
want off in the Scotch-Irish settlement
areas of West Virginia and western North
Carolina. See Marckwardt, "*Want* with el-
lipsis of verbs of motion," *American
Speech* 23(1948), 3-9.
Marckwardt's conclusion is compatible
also with the marked regional pattern in
the UM. Want off is almost entirely confined to the areas not only of Midland
but also of South Midland influence,
i.e., southern Iowa and Nebraska. Fur-
thermore, of the four infs. using want
off in Northern speech territory in Minnesota and North Dakota two, 3 and 205,
have a Scottish background and neither of
the others has a German background. Want
off exhibits only a regional contrast;
where it is found it occurs on all social
and educational levels.

	Type I	Type II	Type III
want off	17%	20%	25%
want to get off	83%	80%	81%

	Mn.	Ia.	N.D.	S.D.	Nb.	Ave.
want off	3%	39%	8%	8%	36%	19%
want to get off	97%	65%	92%	88%	64%	82%

want off sn3, ¹57, 65; 109, 115, 117, 119, 124-25, 128, 130-31, 133-36, 138-39, 142-43, 148, 150; 205, 221; 303, s308, ¹310, 316; f403, 404, 406, 410, 412, 416-17, 423-24, 426-28, 431-32.

want to get off 1-26, 28-33, f34, 35-64; 101-8, 110-14, 116, 119-21, *122, 123, 126-27, 129, 132, 137, 140-41, 144-47, 149-50; 201-4, 206-20, c222, 223-26; 301-2, 304, 306-7, 309-14, 317-28; 401-2, f403, 405, 407-9, 411, 413-15, 418-22, 425-26, 429, 433-37.

no response 27; 118, 151-52; 305, 315; 430.

Comment:

want off: "Southern expression"—57. Usu.—150.

An occasional question to an inf. early in the UM fieldwork aroused the suspicion that want off and the similar want in and want out, as in "The dog wants in," do not have the same frequency of occurrence. Although want in was not officially included at the time as a worksheet item, fws. subsequently asked about it enough so as to produce data supporting that suspicion.

Eight Iowa infs. reported as using the full want to get off have only the elliptical want in or want out, as do five North Dakota infs. and 14 South Dakota infs. In Nebraska 19 of the infs. who say

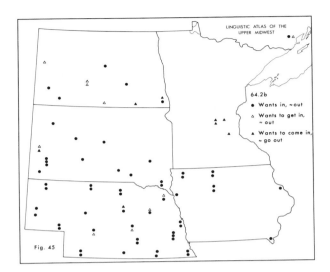

Fig. 45

want to get off have only want in or want out.

Although the somewhat casual attention paid to want in by the fws. did not yield a full picture, three conclusions can be drawn: want in is even more frequent than want off; it is largely restricted to the area of Midland speech; and it reveals no social or educational preference.

want in sn3; 101-4, 111-13, 119; 211, 214-15; 301-2, 311-12, 314, 320-21, 324, 326-27; 401-2, c403, 404, 408-12, 417-18, 423-24, c428, 429, 431, c434, 436. want out 150; 219, 226; 312-13, 322, 325; c403, 405-6, 414, 416, 420, 422, 425-27, 432-33, 435, 437.

want to come in 38; 224-25. want to go out 29-31; 310; 413.

want to get in sn3; 210, 216-17; 309; 407. want to get out 223; 415, 419, 421.

no response 1-2, 4-28, 32-37, 39-65; 105-10, 114-18, 120-49, 151-52; 201-9, 212-13, 218, 220-23; 303-8, 315-19, 323, 328; 430.

rather

63.3 It's rather cold.

Several limiting adverbs, not precisely synonymous, modify cold in this context. Malmstrom notes that although rather is fairly strong in New England, especially among the cultivated infs., it is weaker elsewhere, giving ground to either of two forms both of which are scorned in school textbooks. One, kind of (often actualized as /kaɪndə/), is the majority term in all the eastern dialect project areas and in the North Central states. The other, sort of /sɔrtə/, has only a scattered 6% fre-

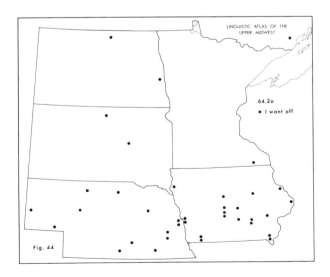

Fig. 44

quency in New England but 24% in the Middle Atlantic states, 40% in the South Atlantic region, and 20% in the North Central area.

The UM data reveal rather retaining its minority status, with greater frequency among the more highly schooled infs.; kind of is the majority form in all the UM states but Iowa. There, sort of, consistently with its Midland and South Midland bias, is the choice of nearly one inf. in four. Although kind of is slightly favored proportionately by the less educated, this is not true of sort of; and for neither of them do any infs. overtly express an attitude reflecting the disapproval of textbook writers.

Of other minor variants only pretty appears with any significant frequency, and then with its greater proportion among the better educated infs.

	Type I	Type II	Type III
kind of	67%	60%	31%
a little	3%	9%	13%
pretty	4%	15%	31%
rather	19%	27%	31%
sort of	11%	18%	19%

	Mn.	Ia.	N.D.	S.D.	Nb.	Ave.
kind of	80%	40%	58%	71%	78%	66%
a little	5%	4%	12%	0	14%	7%
pretty	16%	9%	8%	4%	14%	11%
rather	20%	21%	42%	21%	22%	24%
sort of	14%	23%	15%	4%	11%	15%

a bit 37.
kind of s1, c3, 4-5, sn6-7, 9, c11, sn12, c13-16, 19, c20, 21-23, :26, 27, s28, c29, 30, c31, c35, :c36, s37, c38, sn41, c44, f45, c46-47, 49-52, sn54, c55, c59, 60, c61-63, 64; 101-4, 107-9, 111-12, 114-15, c120, 121, 123, 128, c135, 136-37, s139, 145; 203-4, 206, 208, c209, 210, c211, 212, c214, 215-17, c220, c224-26; c301-2, 303-4, 309, s310, c311, sn312, 313, c314, 315, 321, c322, 323-24, c325, 326, c327, 328; c401, 402-3, c404-5, 406-7, sn408, c409, 410, 412, c414, 415-16, c417, sn418, 419, 421, cvr422, c423, 426, c427, 428, c429, c432-33, sn435, 436-37.
a little 42, 48, 58; 131, 141; 215, 219, 223; 410, 428, 433, sn435. a little bit 430.
middlin' 113, 132. a mite 37. moderately 131.
pretty 9, 12, 34, 43, 45, 53, 57-58, 60, 65; 110-11, 121, 137; 205, 217; 305; 419-20, 423, 425, c426.
quite 2, 33, 54; 101, 105, 122; 305, cvr314; 419, 433.
rather c3, 8, 10, sn12, 21-22, 32-33, s37, 39, sn41, 42, sn54, s¹58, 65; 104, s108, 110, 116, 119-20, 125-26, ?129,

134, s137, s139, 147-48, s150; c201, 202-4, 207, 212-13, c219, 221-22, 226; 308, 310, 312, c318, s320, 326; 403, 406, c409, 411, s425, 430-31, 434-35.
slightly 319. somewhat 435.
sort of 9, c13, 17, c18, 24, 40, ¹44, c47, sn54, c59; 102, s106, 117, 121, s124, c127, 130, s?131, 133, 138, 142-44, s150, c152; 205, 218-19, 221; 320; c414, 422, s424, s427, cvr431, sn435.
too 56.
no response 25; 118, 140, 146, 149, 151; 306-7, 316-17; 413.

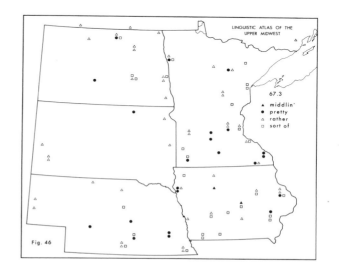

Comment:
kind of: Usu.—22, 60. Not so cold as 'pretty'—217. rather: Not so cold as 'pretty'—65. Usu.—435. too: Inf. insists he says 'too' and not 'rather,' 'pretty,' or 'kind of'—56.

this way

41.4 Do it this way!

This item, not used in the major eastern surveys, was included in the later generalized worksheets that provided the basis for those used in the North Central states and the UM. It is intended to reveal the extent of the occurrence of the -a- or epenthetic /ə/ in the adverbial phrase this way.
Standard this way is nearly universal in the UM. This-a-way occurs as a relic in the speech of only 14 (14%) of the responding Type I infs., two (2.5%) of the Type II's and none of the Type III's, as follows: 1, c27, 36-37, 56, c59; c103, c107, c132, c142, *146, 147; c216, c223;

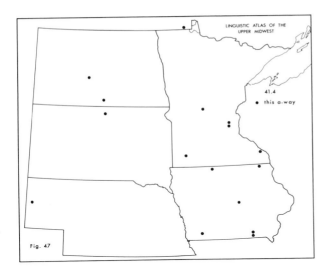

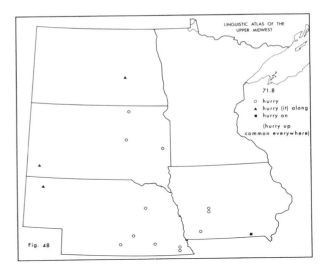

303; c409. Inf. 128 reports it as found in his community.

Since one-half of the instances are in free conversation, it may well be that an inf. who responds to a completion question with a careful this way will use this-a-way in ordinary speech. If so, the latter expression is more common than the data suggest.

This-a-way seems not to have been carried west very successfully. In the North Central state of Wisconsin 22% of the infs. have it; in Minnesota only 10%; in North Dakota 8%. Twelve of the 16 UM instances are in the two eastern states, Minnesota and Iowa.

(hurry) up!

71.8 hurry up!

Not sought in New England or the North Central states and added in the UM only after the Minnesota investigation, this item purports to ascertain the spread of hurry on!—presumably South Midland—into Iowa and Nebraska.

Although several lexical equivalents turned up, only one inf., in southern Iowa, uses this term. Three western infs. have hurry along! The almost universal expression is hurry up! with simple hurry! found in an area embracing southwestern Iowa and the eastern portions of Nebraska and·South Dakota.

come on 312. come on along 307. get a move on 418.
hurry 126-27, 142; 305, 316, 319; 416, 423, 431-32, 434-35. hurry along 320; 402. hurry it along 219. hurry on 147.

hurry up 29-31, 35-36, 38; 101-17, 119-24, s126, 127-41, 143-50, 152; 201-2, c203, 204-26; 301-4, 306, 308-14, !315, 316-19, sn320, 321-25, 327-28; 401-6, :407, 408, 410-15, 417-30, 433, 436-37. hurry it up 125.

shake it up 436. speed 'er up 409. step on it 126; 307. time's a-wasting 409. walk up 145. whip up a little 141.

no response 1-28, 32-34, 37, 39; 118, 151; 326.

yonder

41.3 It's over yonder. NE 707.

To indicate a middle distance between "here" and "far away," infs. typically

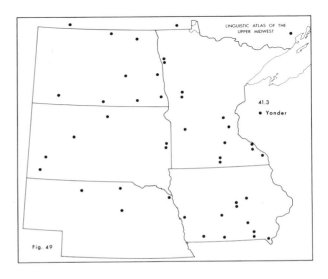

use <u>over there</u>. It occurs throughout New England, although in the northern sector it is less common than <u>over yonder</u>, an expression even at the time of the New England study considered by younger infs. there to be old-fashioned.

In the UM <u>over there</u> is even stronger. <u>Over yonder</u> persists with some vitality among the older infs., except in Nebraska, but it clearly is receding. No college graduates use it, and only half as many Type II's as Type I's. As in New England, <u>yonder</u> is sometimes held to be older or no longer in use. A number of speakers have both terms.

An occasional equivalent, such as <u>down yonder</u>, is likewise reported, along with a few instances of single <u>yonder</u>.

	Type I	Type II	Type III
there	80%	87%	100%
yonder	30%	17%	0

	Mn.	Ia.	N.D.	S.D.	Nb.	Ave.
there	78%	84%	85%	77%	100%	85%
yonder	23%	22%	35%	23%	11%	23%

back there 119; 413, 428. down there c17; c115.
  down yonder †127.
  over nigh ɪ†25.
  over that way 315. over the way 63.
  over there 2-6, 9-12, c13, 14, c15-17, 18, 21-24, c25, 26-30, 32-34, 38-39, 42-47, 49-50, c51-52, 53-55, c57, 59-61, 64-65; 101-8, c109, 110-12, 114, 116-18, s120, 121-23, 125-26, 128-30, 132, c133, 134-35, 137-44, 148; 201-5, 207-17, 219-23, 226; 301-2, 304-10, 312-14, :321, 322-26, 328; 401-7, 409-12, c413, 414-15, 417-23, 425-29, c430, 432-37.
  over yonder 1, 3, 7-8, †11, sn19, 20, ɪ†25, sɪ26, 31, sɪ34, †35, 37, †39, s†40, 41, ɪ47, 48, ɪ50, 54-56, 62-63; 124, 136, 142, 145, sn149; sn201, 204, †205, 206, 215, ɪ216, 218, †219, sn220, 223, sn224, 225; sn302, 303, sɪ309, ɪ310, 311, ɪ313, 317-18, 320, †322; 404-5, sn407, s412, 414.
  there c15, 58; 131; 416, 424.
  up there c13; 113; 319.
  up yonder c132.
  way down there 319. way off there 40.
  way yonder c133.
  yonder 118, 130, sɪ†135, s†144, 146-47.
  no response 36; 150-52; 316, 327; 408, 431.

Comment:
  down <u>yonder</u>: "Old word that has kind've been throwed away"—127. <u>over nigh</u>: Formerly used by German people here—25. <u>over yonder</u>: Used by inf.'s father (from Maine)—11. Formerly used by German people here—25. "There's a few women here who say that once in a while"—26. Used by older people and southerners—34. Inf. says this is an "eastern" expression; heard from her father's relatives (from Maine)—40. Heard from older or "illiterate" people—50. Inf. says 'over yonder' means further away than 'over there'—55; 414. Used by inf.'s father (from Ontario)—205. Used by inf.'s father (from England)—219.

CHAPTER 10

Syntactic Miscellany

look here!

54.3 <u>Look here!</u> NE 596.

The basic imperative <u>Look here!</u> is used to attract attention to an object or situation or idea, particularly one that is new or different. It has several syntactic variants.

All variants appear both in New England and in the UM. Less favored by the less educated is simple <u>Look here!</u> Only six out of 10 Type I infs. use it, but three-fourths of the Type II's and all but one of the college graduates do.

<u>Look-it-here!</u> (perhaps derived from <u>look at plus</u> an object) has clear Northern orientation and is less favored by the educated. Only one college graduate, an Iowan, uses it.

A marked regional pattern appears also with two related variants characterized by an epenthetic vowel, perhaps reduced from earlier at. <u>Look-a-here!</u> has /ə/ and <u>Looky-here!</u> has /ɪ/. Although obviously related, and similar in that both have Midland orientation, they are distinguished by some difference in both regional and social distribution. <u>Look-a-here!</u> has apparently won somewhat higher acceptance from Northern speakers, mostly in Type I, but <u>Looky-here!</u> has won somewhat greater acceptance from the better educated in the area where it is found.

	Type I	Type II	Type III
Look here!	60%	75%	93%
Look-it-here!	12%	11%	7%
Look-a-here!	20%	9%	0
Looky-here!	10%	13%	7%

	Mn.	Ia.	N.D.	S.D.	Nb.	Ave.
Look here!	82%	72%	58%	42%	64%	66%
Look-it-here!	10%	4%	29%	21%	6%	11%
Look-a-here!	10%	13%	8%	21%	22%	13%
Looky-here!	0	21%	4%	5%	22%	10%

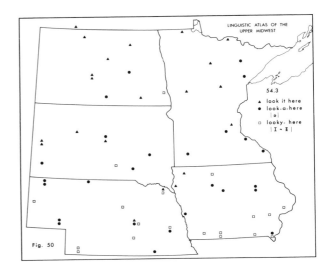

Fig. 50

look here /lʊk hɪr/ 1-3, 6, sn7, 9-11, 14, 17, f18, 20-22, !23, 24-25, sn26, 27-28, sn29, 30-34, 36-40, sn41, 42-43, !44, 45-47, 49-50, c51, 52-53, 55, 57-58, 60-65; 101, 103, cr?104, 105-6, 109-12, 115, 118-19, 121-23, 125-27, 129-34, 136-38, sn139, 141, 143, 145-46, 148-50; 204, →205, 206-10, 213-15, 219-22; 301, 303-4, c311, †312, ¹313, 323, 325-26, 328; 404-6, 410-16, 418-19, 422-23, 425-28, 430-33, 435.

look-it-here /lʊk ɪt hɪr/ 4, *5, ¹7, sn10, 19, c21, 37; 102, 110; 201, 203, †205, 211-12, 216-17, 224; 302, 309-10, 315; 407, 420.

look-a-here /lʊk ə hɪr/ [ə] 13, c15, 35, sn†48, 54, c56, 59; 113-14, 116-17, 124, 149; !¹206, 218, 223; ¹313, 314, 320, 322, 327; sn!401, 402-3, 417, 421, ¹422, 425, 433, 436.

looky-here /lʊk ɪ hɪr/ [iˇ~iˇ~ɪ^~ɪˀ~ +ˁ~+] 104, 127, 135, 140, c142, 144, *145, 147, 150, !152; 225; 321; 408-9, 414, 421, sn423, 424, 429, 437.

no response 8, 12, 16; 107-8, 120, 128, 151; 202, 226; 305-8, 316-19, 324; 434.

Comment:

look here: A reprimand; 'look it here' used to call attention—110. Used to call attention; 'look-a-here' used as a reprimand—149. look-a-here: An exclamation; 'look here' used as a directive—425. look it here: Always used by inf.'s father—10. Usu.—21. looky-here: "Dad always said, 'looky-here'"—127. Used to call attention; 'look-a-here' used to retain attention—421.

don't you touch it!

71.5 Don't you touch it! NE 689.

As an imperative warning to a child, this injunction appears in three variant expressions in the UM. They offer a sharp contrast to the situation in New England. The major New England form is minor in the UM; conversely, the minor New England form is the principal one in the UM.

Simple Don't touch! is a minor variant not reported at all in New England, used by only four infs. in Wisconsin, but found in the speech of 44 UM infs., more than one-half of whom are in North Dakota. Its nonappearance in northern Iowa may result from the practice of fw. H.

Don't touch it (or, that, them, etc.) dominates the UM, with its greatest frequency in Nebraska. In New England, however, it is a distinct minority form characteristic of the southern portion. Of the 62 instances in New England none occurs in Maine and only five each in New Hampshire and Vermont. More than one-half of the remaining 52 are in the southwestern area, i.e., Connecticut and that part of Massachusetts west of the Connecticut River.

Don't you touch it, typically /dont ʃʊ tʌtʃ ɪt/, is the least common of the three variants. Although it is easily the dominant form in Massachusetts, it apparently has become sharply recessive in Northern speech, for its UM occurrence is chiefly in Midland territory, i.e., Iowa and Nebraska. Further evidence of its Northern decline appears in the fact that only two instances are reported in the Wisconsin survey.

	Type I	Type II	Type III
Don't touch!	17%	22%	37%
Don't touch it!	70%	67%	63%
Don't you touch it!	11%	10%	6%

	Mn.	Ia.	N.D.	S.D.	Nb.	Ave.
Don't touch!	15%	16%	54%	20%	14%	20%
Don't touch it!	80%	71%	62%	72%	56%	70%
Don't you touch it!	3%	14%	0	4%	30%	10%

Don't touch! 1, 5, 11, 17, 20, 31, 33, 35, !45, 60; 122-23, 127, 131, 134, 149-50, 152; 202, 204, 206-8, 211, 213, 216-18, 221, 224-26; 304, 308, 319-20, 324; 402, 409-10, 421, 426.

Don't touch it! 2, c3, 4, 6-10, 12-15, c16, 18-19, 21-32, 34, 36-43, c44, 49-56, 58-59, 61-65; 101-6, 108-15, 117, 119-21, 124-26, 128-29, 132-33, 136-38, 141-42, 144-48; 201, 203, 205, 209-10, 212, 214-15, 219-20, 222-23; 301-3, 306-7, 309-13, 315-16, 318, 321-23, 325-26; 401, 403-6, :407, 408, 411-13, 415, 417-20, 424-25, 429-30, 437.

Don't you touch it! 48, 57; 107, 116, 130, 139-40, 143, sn150; 305; 414, 416, 422-23, 427-28, 431-35.

Don't you dare touch that! !47. Don't you, no ¹205. Mustn't touch! 46. Never touch those! c13. Touch, touch! 317.

no response 118, 135, 151; 314, 327-28; 436.

nor I either

54.5 Nor I either. NE 612.

After such a remark as "I'm not going to do it," infs. in both New England and the UM indicate a similar reaction by a variety of responses.

In the UM the sought response, Nor I either, comes from about one-third of the infs. in Minnesota, Iowa, and North Dakota, but from only a few in South Dakota

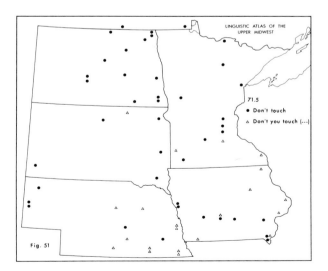

71.5
• Don't touch
△ Don't you touch (---)

LINGUISTIC ATLAS OF THE UPPER MIDWEST

Fig. 51

and Nebraska. The corresponding multiple negative, <u>Nor I neither</u>, is offered only by less-educated speakers in Minnesota and Iowa. Related <u>Me</u> (n)<u>either</u> is similarly rejected by <u>college graduates</u> but is more widely scattered.

The various responses appear below.

I'm not either 31, 37; 102, 104, 107, 109, 121, 126, 134, 145, 147, 152; 203, 214, 224; 402, 409-11, 414, 420, 424. I ain't either 113, 135, 142. I can't either 309; 437. I don't either c14, 38; 323-25, 327; 406, 418-19, 429. I won't either 5, 9-10, :29, 36, 56; 105-6, 110, 112, 115-17, 122, 124, 127, 129-30, 136-37, 144, 150; 212, 217, 219, 223, 225-26; 306, 317, 320, 326; 401, 403, 417, 421, f422, 430. I wouldn't either 146, 148; 213; 301, 312; 405.

I don't neither 328; 436. I won't neither 138, 143; 404.

neither am I 21, 47, 54-55, 62; 101, 103, 125, 128, 141, 149; 210; 313, 318. neither do I 22; 303. neither will I 17-19, 30, 34, 45, 53, 58; 108, 131, 136, 140; 216, 221, 224; 304, 310, 319, 326. neither would I 408-9, 412.

nor I either 8, 20, 23, 25, 32, 40, ?41, 43-46, 50-52, 60-61, 64-65; 101, 104, 109-11, 114-15, 120, sn133, 137; 205, 209, 211, 215, 218, 220; 302, 319; 411. nor me either 202.

nor I neither 7, †40, 46, ?59, 62-63. nor neither I 39. nor neither am I sn139. nor me neither 118.

or I either 26.

me either 204; 308; s425. me neither 12, 48, 57; 119; :201; 308; 423, 433, 435.

nor I 33, s34, 53, ?58; 208; 317; 426. nor am I 316, 318. nor will I 34.

not me 416, c428, 431. or me 425.

no response 1-4, 6, 11, 13, 15-16, 24, 27-28, 35, 42, 49; 123, 132, 151; 206-7, 222; 305, 307, ?311, 314-15, 321-22; 407, 413, 415, 427, 432, 434.

Comment:
neither will I: Usu.—53. nor I either: More formal than 'I'm not either'—411. nor I neither: "Improper"—40.

CHAPTER 11

Addenda

Besides obtaining information from responses to the grammatical items in the worksheets, fws. were asked to note other grammatical matters likely to concern a student of American regional English. Such notations, however, were not made systematically, as fws. varied in their personal interests and in their readiness to draw upon forms appearing in free conversation.

A clear social distribution is evident in the fact that nearly all of the various language instances noted below occur in the conversation of Type I infs. and hence are in a usage range that can be termed nonstandard.

But, although as with any more an occasional regional correlation can be inferred, the expressions were collected too unsystematically to be useful in ascertaining the existence of regional distribution patterns. They are given here, however, as recorded data better preserved than discarded.

VERBS

Tense Forms

Ask. The preterit of ask appears as ast /æst/ in the speech of the following, four in Type I, one in Type II, and one in Type III: 29, 35; 322; 417, 422, 431.

Bear. The participle, or participial adjective, as in "I was born in 1896," appears as borned in the speech of inf. 303.

Break. For the following six Type I infs. and three Type II infs. the past participle is broke: 22, 25, 31; 109; 301, 303; 414, 418, 436.

Drag. Drug is the past tense for inf. 139 and the participle for inf. 322, both in Type I.

Draw. Drawed is the preterit for infs. 31, 322, and 407, and the participle for inf. 139, all of whom are in Type I.

Fly. For Type I inf. 25 the preterit of this verb appears in "He flied off."

Go. For 12 Type I infs. and 7 Type II's the past participle of go is went: 21, 31; 109, 112, 121, 138; .209, 212, 215; 307, 314, 316, 322; 402, 404, 416, 423, 429-30. Inf. 138 also has went in "We'd a like to went," where it probably is the participle and not the infinitive.

Keep. The loss of the second member of the /pt/ consonant cluster of kept in the speech of some infs. has led to their accepting the vowel change from /kɪp/ to /kɛp/ as signaling the preterit tense. In surface grammar keep for them has become a strong verb. Kep /kɛp/ was heard in the speech of the following five Type I infs. and three Type II's: 201, 225; 301, 311, 325; 402, 404, 429.

Know. An analogically regular preterit form knowed /nod/ appears in the speech of four Type I infs. and one Type II: 35; 118; 311-12, 322. Knowed is the participle for these Type I infs.: 303, 322; 407.

Reach. Inf. 429 has the preterit rech /rɛtʃ/.

Ruin. Inf. 35 has the preterit ruint.

Sing. Two Type I infs. have sang as the participle.

Sleep. As with keep, above, the loss of -t has created a new strong preterit slep /slɛp/ as evidenced in the speech of five Type I infs. and one Type II: 31, 37; 208, 225; 322; 429.

Swear. Inf. 429 has swore as the past participle.

Present Indicative

Two Type I speakers have -s as an ending in the first person: "So I goes to work"—220; "I says to one of the guards"—314.

Number and Concord

A plural subject with a singular verb form appears in the conversation of four Type I infs. and three Type II's: "Them three spiders is"—35; "There was 32 set down at the table"—202; "Fireplaces is out"—225; "Some of 'em spouts quite often"—314; "Our pigs was there"—402; "Them things is bad"—405; "Them is"—432.

Phrases

Used to could, as a phrase equivalent to standard used to be able, occurs in the conversation of three Type I infs. and one Type II: "I used to could remember a few words of Welsh"—21; "I used to could call them things"—35; "We used to could have fun"—211; "You used to could set your watch by it"—314.

Inf. 215 also has the expression found in "You couldn't use to fool me."

Prepositional Verb

Three Type I infs. have the prepositional verb remember of instead of simple remember: "I don't remember of it"—31; 311; "I don't remember of having to use it"—314.

NOUNS

Number

One inf., 36, has the analogical plural sheeps.

One inf., 13, has a singular lynk by back-formation from lynx. Similarly, cactus is treated as a plural by inf. 214 in the locution "in those cactus," and fox, likewise, by inf. 303 in "The fox are comin' in."

Group Genitive

One group genitive appears in the free conversation of a Type II inf.: "He [a dog] was the boy that's home's dog"—203.

PRONOUNS

Case Form

The first-person plural pronoun used with a following noun (usually kids in the citations) in close apposition appears in subject position as us in the conversation of six Type I infs. and two Type II's: "So us kids wouldn't mess it up"—11; "Us kids stood around and bellered"—31; ". . . after us youngsters went to school"—209; "Us kids" (as subject)—216; "Us kids seen 'em"—224; ". . . a trick that us goddamned snot-nosed kids used to do"—311; "Us kids thought . . ."—420; "Us kids 'd been raised"—436.

In object position the same construction yielded we for inf. 409: ". . . to coax we kids."

In subject position, with quasi-demonstrative force, the third-person plural pronoun appears as them in the speech of three Type I infs. and one Type II: "Them are funny questions"—220; "I don't think them are called spiderwebs"—324; "Them is . . ."—432; "Them's the ones"—436.

For three Type III speakers them also serves as the equivalent of the standard demonstrative those with adjectival function in both subject and object positions: "Them three spiders is . . ."—35; "I saw them seeds"—220; "Them things is hard." "Them kind of barns"—405.

As a member of a compound noun phrase a personal pronoun appears in the nonstandard case form in both subject and object positions. As subject, it appears with six Type I infs. and one Type II: "Him and Scott used to be great pals"—21; "Him and my older sister were . . ."—31; "Him and his wife don't go"—203; "I and her went"—209; "Her and I have been very good friends"—212; "Him and I had a talk"—216; "Me and a bunch of kids"—417. As object, it appears with three Type I infs. and two Type II's: "between he and Kenneth"—211; "I rode back from Yankton with he and his wife"—314; "He met my father and I going to town"—322; "like you and I"—413; "They didn't want my brother and I to know"—419.

Introductory There

Both they and it appear as nonstandard replacements of existential there. Three Type I infs. have they: "They ain't no creeks named here"—220; "They was a fight"—413; "They was two of 'em"—418. One Type II speaker has it: "It wasn't any roof"—430. Further evidence may make significant the fact that the preceding four instances occur in Midland speech territory.

Those kind of

In accord with a feeling that kind of constitutes a syntactic adjectival phrase modifying a following plural noun, the demonstrative pronoun that, when used adjectivally before kind of, appears as those with six Type I infs. and two Type

II's: "those kind of contraptions"—11; "more of those kind of people"—31; "those kind of books"—208; "those kind of things"—317; 401, 414, 424; "those kind of people"—422. One inf., 405, has them in the same construction: "them kind of barns."

Reflexives

Two nonstandard reflexive forms occur. Type I inf. 403 has theirselves, and Type II inf. 436 has "to hide themself."

ADVERBIALS

Three infs. in Midland speech territory have adjectives functioning as adverbs: "It hurt terrible." "He was fined heavy"—121; "I like it tol'able hard"—132; "very easy done"—138.

Forwhy, classified as obsolete in the *Oxford English Dictionary* and as archaic in the Merriam-Webster *Third New International Dictionary* and other current dictionaries, appears in the remark "That's forwhy he kep the other girl," uttered by a Type I Canadian inf., 201, both of whose parents were born in England.

ADJECTIVE AND ADVERB COMPARISON

Two Type I infs. in Midland territory have double comparison: "to be more nicer in their speech"—314; "ash burns more cleaner"—427. One Type II, 121, has beautifulest for more beautiful.

PREPOSITION

The preposition agin /ə'gɪn/, from archaic again, is used by seven Type I infs. and two Type II's: 132, 138-39; 204; 314; 404-5, 427, 429. Perhaps significant is the fact that all but one of the infs. live in Midland speech territory; the exception, 204, is of British parentage.

MULTIPLE NEGATION

Instances of multiple negation occur in the conversation of 49 infs., 36 in Type

I, 12 in Type II, and one in Type III. One instance has three negatives: "I don't never want to see that no more"—35. All others have two.

Most instances of double negation appear in the pattern not + verb + either a negative pronoun or no + noun. Typical contexts are "They ain't got no horses"—25; "They don't need nothin' much"—31; "That doesn't improve nobody's property"—201; "That won't make no biscuits"—212; "I didn't tell them no definite thing"—316; "She ain't got no husband"—317; "That ain't no creek"—417; ". . . didn't have no separate room"—434. Infs. providing examples of this kind are 7, 25, 27, 31, 35, 39-40, 46, 51, 62-63; 118, 138-39, 143; 201, 204, 212, 220, 225; 301, 303, 305, 316-17; 402, 404, 415-17, 422, 434, 436.

Another pattern is that of not + verb + the adverbial no more: "I don't bother with it no more"—22; see also the triple negative example above—35; "I don't remember no more"—36; "You don't hear that no more"—209; "They don't do that no more"—314.

Another pattern is that of not + never + verb: "I didn't never"—22; "He ain't never showed"—311; "That's said by an element that hasn't never been to school much"—318; "I don't never remember"—401; "He didn't never think"—427.

Less frequent is the pattern of never + verb + no: "I never pay no attention"—38; "I never had no . . ."—54, 314; "We never had nothin'"—322; "I never heard no voices"—407.

Only one inf. has the combination of a negative preposition followed by no and a noun: "without no roof"—303.

SYNTACTIC MISCELLANY

Any more occurs in affirmative context in the speech of two Type I infs., three Type II's, and one Type III—all of them in Midland speech territory. Had this been sought as a worksheet item, it is almost certain that the resulting data would have a sharp regional distribution, with no instances from Northern speakers. Examples are the following: "Usually any more they're shrunk"—150; "But any more we always say 'frying pan'"—325; "Any more it's a low ceiling"—404; "Any more it doesn't amount to much"—405; context not recorded—412; "That's all we buy any more"—417.

Whether is omitted by one inf. from an indirect question in which the normal inverted order is retained: "I don't know would it be fine enough"—119. This construction, reported more frequently in the South, is characterized by Quirk as "Irish English": Randolph Quirk and Sidney Greenbaum, *A Concise Grammar of Contemporary English* (New York, 1973), 318.

A redundant subject occurs: "My dad he hauled buffalo bones"—209.

The subject relative pronoun is omitted by inf. 212: "There was an Indian woman came along."

Inf. 121 has "My wife is dead about fifteen years."

Inf. 322 has "After he got done with father . . ."

CHAPTER 12

Synopsis

In his survey of eastern verb forms Atwood found both an expected range of social contrasts and also a variety of regional distribution patterns.

The UM, however, reveals a somewhat different situation with respect both to verb forms and also to other grammatical matters appearing in the worksheets. Some of the older minor variants contributing to regional subdialect differences along the Atlantic coast failed to survive during the western migration; others persist so weakly as to be inadequate criterions for geographical patterns. But although the tendency toward leveling has progressed far enough so as to remove a number of minor regional variants, those that remain join major variants as social class markers. With matters of grammar social contrast is hence more conspicuous than is regional contrast. Grammatical differences are largely a function of differences in age and education.

REGIONAL VARIATION

What regional contrast does appear is manifest in two categories. One is consistent with the historical Northern/Midland dialectal split. The other is consistent with the time of population settlement.

A Northern dialect provenience appears, for example, in the distribution of clim, youse, and look-it-here, all occurring in Northern speech territory.

Midland orientation, on the contrary, appears in the proportional distribution in Iowa, Nebraska, and South Dakota of clum, dremp, learnt, spoilt, swum, and tore, as well as of the expressions want off and looky-here.

Infrequently significant minimal sur-

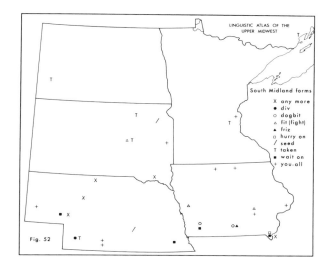

Fig. 52

LINGUISTIC ATLAS OF THE UPPER MIDWEST

South Midland forms
X any more
• div
o dogbit
△ fit (fight)
▲ friz
□ hurry on
/ seed
T taken
■ wait on
+ you-all

vival of South Midland forms is exemplified in the instances of dogbit, div, fit (preterit of fight), friz, seed pret., set/sot correlation, taken pret., srunk, you-all, wait on, hurry on, and the incidental recording of affirmative any more, all of which are reported chiefly in southern Iowa and Nebraska.

That their life is precarious is suggested by the fact that even speakers of South Midland background no longer exhibit consistent use of South Midland terms. Those terms that remain are sporadic last-ditch survivors of the competition with Midland and, sometimes, Northern equivalents. The informant who says you-all is neither a predictable user of, say, hurry on, and certainly not of nonstandard taken, nor even of the South Midland lexical terms described in Volume 1.

A few grammatical forms exhibit the spreading tendency that blurred the re-

83

gional background of many lexical forms. Dove preterit, a distinctly Northern form in the Middle Atlantic and North Central regions, has been so readily adopted by Midland speakers that it is the majority form throughout the UM.

Three terms with strong Midland orientation, on the contrary, have been adopted by Northern speakers to such an extent that in the UM they no longer serve as dialect markers. <u>Fit</u> as a preterit of <u>fit</u> now dominates Minnesota and North Dakota as well as, expectedly, Iowa and Nebraska. Midland <u>rode</u> as the preterit of <u>ride</u> actually is strongest in Minnesota, and Midland <u>seen</u> occurs throughout the five states. The latter two, of course, are nonstandard forms that may eventually yield to the leveling influence of the schools.

It is almost certainly this school influence that preponderantly has led to the second category of regional contrast, that which is consistent with time of settlement. Just as the North Central region, according to Virginia McDavid, exhibits fewer grammatical variations than does the Atlantic coast, so the UM has fewer than does the North Central region. Likewise, within the UM the eastern first settled half, comprising Minnesota and Iowa, exhibits fewer grammatical variations than does the western more recently settled half, comprising the Dakotas and Nebraska.

Presumably the effect of the schools has been strong for a complex of reasons. Two of them are fairly obvious: the removal of the settlers from a broad base of folk speech and the desire of second-generation immigrant children to assimilate.

As people moved farther westward, each generation progressively left farther and farther behind the sturdy local base of folk speech characteristic of the thirteen original states. Only a fairly shallow foundation of folk speech remained for the first and second locally born generations in the new territories. These generations were at once susceptible to the normative grammar teaching of the country school and the community grade school, a teaching directed particularly at variations within the irregular verbs. Such teaching would expectedly have an especially strong and lasting effect upon Type II informants, with their added years of schooling and with some measure of the linguistic insecurity that induces unquestioning acceptance of school grammar rules.

A second reason for the strong school influence surely must have been that in much of the UM an unusual receptiveness to school teaching exists in the children and grandchildren of non-English-speaking parents from Germany, Scandinavia, Bohemia, and elsewhere. Almost without exception these parents sought for their children complete assimilation into their new home, encouraged abandonment of the Old World tongue, and insisted that the children learn "good English," presumably the English of the school grammars. Even with users of nonstandard English in the community, probably even within their peer group, children found the situation less than favorable to the persistence of grammatical features not approved in the schools.

A statistical summary of this normalizing trend will support the generalization. Atwood's *Verb Forms of the Eastern United States* lists 192 verb variants found in the fieldwork in New England and the Atlantic states. Virginia McDavid's 1956 dissertation lists 175 variants in the North Central states. But 14 of these are new, previously unreported, so that actually only 161 of the listed variants survived the first wave of western migration across the Appalachians. Thirty-one variants apparently had been lost during the move.

The rate of attrition increased as people moved westward. Only 93 verb variants are listed in this volume for the UM; i.e., 82 more variants were lost during the second westward movement. In other words, of a total of 206 variants for the east coast and the North Central states, 113 forms did not survive the migration across the Mississippi River into the UM.

Only two forms not school-approved have clearly gained in frequency, <u>drank</u> ppl. and <u>dove</u> pret. Rode ppl. and <u>seen</u> pret. are nonstandard forms that maintain vigor, but almost exclusively within the speech of Type I infs.

This standardizing trend apparent in a contrast of the three dialect atlas regions is manifest even within the UM. Decrease in frequency is revealed in the returns for 11 verbs, all of which are proportionately less frequent in the western states, the Dakotas and Nebraska, than in Minnesota and Iowa: <u>bitten</u>, <u>brung</u> ppl., <u>clim</u>, <u>climb</u> pret., <u>drownded</u>, <u>drunk</u> ppl., <u>fit</u> pret., <u>growed</u> ppl., <u>rode</u> ppl., <u>raised</u> pret., <u>rised</u> pret., <u>swum</u> pret., and <u>wrote</u> ppl. Further confirmation comes from the distribution of six additional verb variants, which appear only in the eastern half of the region with no recorded occurrences at all in Nebraska and the Dakotas: <u>climb</u> pret., <u>drownded</u>, <u>driv</u> pret., <u>druv</u> pret., <u>friz</u>, and <u>sot</u> pret.

SOCIAL VARIATION

Despite the perceptible influence of the schools, both with respect to the contrast mentioned above between East and West and also with respect to the general decline in the number of regional variants, social variation persists. Indeed, there is enough to mark conspicuous social contrasts between, for example, the speech of an informant who customarily can say I clum, I done it, he drownded, I've rode a horse ever since I was a kid, he throwed me, and ain't it? and that of the informant who habitually would say I climbed, I did it, he drowned, I've ridden a horse, he threw me, and isn't it?

Nearly all of the grammatical items described in this section display at least a degree of social variation, some conspicuously. The following table indicates in a general way the relative position of a given form on a rough social scale. The symbols do not represent numerical absolutes but rather suggest the proportional strength of a given form among the three types of speakers. The symbol x = very frequent; the symbol - = moderately frequent; the symbol . = least frequent.

	Type I	Type II	Type III
clum	x	-	
come (pret.)	x	-	
done (pret.)	x	.	
dremp	.		
drank (ppl.)	x	x	-
drove (ppl.)	-	.	
drownded	-		
et (pret. and ppl.)	.		
give (pret.)	x	-	.
growed (pret.)	-	.	
growed (ppl.)	.	.	
kneeled	-	.	.
learned (trans.)	-		
lay (intrans.)	x	-	-
rode (ppl.)	-	.	.
run (pret.)	x	-	.
scairt	-	-	.
seen (pret.)	-	-	.
set (pret. of sit)	-	.	.
sit (pret. of sit)	.		
spoilt (ppl. adj.)	-	.	.
sweated	-	.	
swum (pret.)	-	.	
tore (ppl.)	x	-	.
throwed (ppl.)	-	.	.

	Type I	Type II	Type III
awoke	.	-	-
wakened	.	.	-
woke	x	x	-
wore (ppl.)	-	.	
wrote (ppl.)	-	.	.
was (pl.)	x	-	
here's (pl.)	x	-	
ashes is	-	.	
I ain't	x	-	
ain't I?	x	-	
they ain't	-	.	.
usen't	.	.	
he don't	x	x	-
I (h)ain't done it	-	.	
he ain't	x	-	.
hadn't ought	-	.	.
oughtn't	.	.	.
warn't	-	.	.
a-(verb)ing	-	.	.
bushel (pl.)	x	-	.
pound (pl.)	-	.	
youse (pl.)	.	.	
you-all	-	.	
he's the man that . . .	x	-	.
he's the man who . . .	.	-	x
whose	-	x	x
that his	-	.	.
it wasn't I	.	-	-
it wasn't me	x	x	x
them (adj.)	x	-	
sick at the stomach	-	.	
without (conj.)	.	.	
off'n	.	.	
yonder	-	.	

Two forms not school-approved though now listed as standard variants in recent dictionaries have gained in frequency: drank ppl. and dove pret. The contrary is true of several forms that at one time were considered within the area of social acceptability but now are in some disrepute, if not actually declining in frequency as well: catched, drownded, et, fit, growed, run pret., swum pret., swimmed pret., throwed, tore ppl., wore ppl., write ppl., and wrote ppl.

A review of the grammatical descriptions in this section, both those showing regional contrast and those showing social contrast, points also to the statistically insignificant but linguistically important presence of relic forms obviously well on the road toward disappearance. Nearly all of them are predictably characteristic of the speech of the uneducated and hence are significant social markers.

Relic forms of preterits, participles, and participial adjectives include dog-bit, boilt, brung, catched, clim, div, drinked, driv, druv, fit (fight), friz, heared, rid (ride), raised (rise), rised (rise), seed (see), shrinked, sot (sit), taken (take), tuck (take), and took ppl.

Other relics that are treated in this chapter include be as a finite verb, /duz/ for does, for to tell, yourn, hisn, without conj., all to once, to home, sick in the stomach, sick on the stomach, off'n, a-purpose, this-a-way, and yonder.

Index

Index

a- 43-45, 85
a(n) (article) 60
a little (intensive) 73
after (prep.) 68-69
after (him) 63
agin = again 81
ain't (neg. 1st sg. pres. of *be*) 37, 85
(neg. 3d sg. pres. of *be*) 41
(neg. 3d pl. pres. of *be*) 39, 85
ain't (I)? = am not (neg. interrog. 1st sg.) 38, 85
ain't (neg. 1st sg. pres. of *have*) 41, 85
all at once 63
all gone 58
all to once 63, 86
Allen, Harold B. 14
am (1st sg. pres.) 33
am not (neg. 1st sg.) 36
am (I) not? (neg. interrog. 1st sg.) 38
/ant/ (I)? (neg. interrog. 1st sg.) 38
any more (aff.) 81, 83
anyplace 70. F42, 70
anywhere(s) (adv.) 70. F42, 70
a-purpose 70-71, 86. F43, 71
are (sg.) 33, 36. F23, 36
(pl.) 36-37. F24, 37
are not (neg. 3d pl.) 39
aren't (I)? (neg. interrog. 1st sg.) 38
as far as 70
as if (conj.) 61-62

as though (conj.) 61-62
ashes is 85
ask (inf.) 79
ast (pret. of *ask*) 79
at (once) 63
at (the stomach) 64-65, 85
at home 64
ate (pret.) 17. F7, 17
Atwood, E. Bagby 4, 9-10, 12, 14-15, 17, 19, 21, 31, 33, 39, 42, 43, 44, 84
Avis, Walter S. 14
awake (inf.) 31
awaken (inf.) 31
awoke (pret.) 31, 85

back of (the door) 65
be (inf.) 32
(pres.) 33, 86
bear (inf.) 79
beautifulest 81
because (conj.) 61
been (pret.) 33-34. F22, 33
began (pret.) 8
begin (inf.) 8
(pret.) 8
begun (pret.) 8
behind (the door) 65-66
bit (ppl.) 8
bite (inf.) 8
bitten (ppl.) 6, 84
blew (pret.) 9
blow (inf.) 9
blowed (pret.) 9. F1, 9
(ppl.) 9
boil (inf.) 9
boiled (pret.) 9
boilt (ppl.) 9, 86
borned (ppl. adj.) 79
bought (ppl.) 10

boughten (ppl. adj.) 10
break (inf.) 79
bring (inf.) 9
broke (ppl.) 79
brought (ppl.) 9
brung (ppl.) 9, 84, 86
bushel(s) (pl.) 50-51, 85
buy (inf.) 10

cactus (pl.) 80
came (pret.) 11-12
(ppl.) 12
catch (inf.) 10
catched (pret.) 10, 85-86
caught (pret.) 10
clim (pret.) 10-11, 83-84, 86. F2, 11
(ppl.) 10-11. F3, 11
climb (inf.) 10
(pret.) 11, 84. F3, 11
climbed (pret.) 10-11
(ppl.) 10-11
clum (pret.) 10-11, 83, 85. F2, 11
(ppl.) 10-11. F3, 11
come (inf.) 11
(pret.) 12, 85
commence (inf.) 8
commenced (pret.) 8

Dictionary of Contemporary American Usage 47
did (pret.) 13
(ppl.) 13
didn't use to (neg.

3d sg. pret.) 39-40
died from/of/with 66
died of 66
died with 66. F39, 66
div 12, 83, 86. F52, 83
dive (inf.) 12
dived (pret.) 12
do (inf.) 13, 33
(3d sg. pres.) 33
does /dʌz/ (3d sg. pres.) 33
does /duz/ (3d sg. pres.) 33
doesn't (neg. 3d sg. pres.) 40
dogbit (ppl. from *bite*) 8, 83, 86. F52, 83
done (pret.) 13, 85
done (completive verb) 46
don't (neg. 3d sg. pres.) 40, 85
don't touch! 77. F51, 77
don't touch it! 77
don't you touch it! 77. F51, 77
dove (pret.) 12-13, 84
down from = off 68. F41, 68
down yonder 75
drag (inf.) 79
drank (pret.) 14-15
(ppl.) 14-15, 84-85
draw (inf.) 79
drawed (pret.) 79
dream (inf.) 13
dreamed (pret.) 13-14
dreamt (pret.) 13-14
dremp (pret.) 13-14, 83, 85. F4, 13
drimp (pret. of *dream*) 14. F4, 13
drink (inf.) 14

drinked (pret.) 14-15, 86
driv (pret.) 15, 84, 86
drive (inf.) 15
drived (pret.) 15
driven (ppl.) 15-16
drove (pret.) 15 (ppl.) 15-16, 85. F5, 15
drown (inf.) 16 (ppl.) 16. F6, 16
drownded (pret.) 16, 84-85
drowned (ppl.) 16
drug (pret. of *drag*) 79
drunk (pret.) 14-15 (ppl.) 14-15, 84
drunken (ppl.) 15
druv (pret.) 15, 84, 86
/duz/ = does 86

eat (inf.) 16 (pret.) 17-18. F7, 17 (ppl.) 17-18. F8, 17
eaten (ppl.) 17-18
et (pret.) 17, 85. F7, 17 (ppl.) 17-18, 85. F8, 17

fit (inf.) 18 (pret.) 18, 83. F52, 83
fit (pret. of *fight*) 18, 84, 86
fitted (pret.) 18-19. F9, 18
flied (pret. of *fly*) 79
fly (inf.) 79
for (him) 63. F36, 63
(wait) for 66
for to tell (inf. of purpose) 45, 86
forwhy 81
fought (pret.) 18
freeze (inf.) 19
friz 19, 83, 86. F52, 83
from = off 68
from (the stomach) 65
(died) from 66
froze (pret.) 19 (ppl.) 19
frozen (ppl.) 19

gave (pret.) 19 (ppl.) 19
give (inf.) 19 (pret.) 19, 85
go (inf.) 79
Greenbaum, Sidney 82
grew (pret.) 19-20 (ppl.) 19-20
grow (inf.) 19
growed (pret.) 19-20. F10, 20 (ppl.) 20, 84-85. F10, 20
grown (ppl.) 19-20

hadn't ought = ought not (neg. sg.) 42-43. F26, 42
hain't (neg. 1st sg. of *have*) 41
half after (seven) 68-69
half past (seven) 68-69
/hausɪz/ = houses 48
/hauzɪz/ = houses 48
have (inf.) 33
have /v/ or /əv/ 33
have not (neg. 1st sg. pres.) 40-41
he (obj.) 80
he (redundant) 82
hear (inf.) 20
heard (ppl.) 20
heared (ppl.) 20, 86
heat (inf.) 20
heated (pret.) 20 (ppl.) 20
here's (pl.) 85
hern = hers 54-55. F31, 54
hers (3d sg. fem.) 54
het (pret. of *heat*) 20 (ppl.) 20
him and I 80
his (3d sg. masc.) 54
hisn = his 54-55, 86. F31, 54
home = at home 64
hoofs (pl.) 47
hooves (pl.) 47. F28, 47
horseshoe(s) (the game) 47-48
houses (pl.) 48
hurry! 74. F48, 74
hurry along! 74. F48, 74
hurry on! 74. F48, 74
hurry up! 74

I (1st sg. post-*be*) 56-57, 85
(want) in 72. F45, 72
in (the stomach) 65
in back of (the door) 65
in/into 66
-ing /ɪŋ/ or /ɪn/ 43-45
is (3d pl. of *be*) 33, 36-37, 80. F24, 37
isn't (neg. 1st sg. pres.) 41
it = there 80

Jespersen, Otto 14

keep (inf.) 79
kep (pret.) 79
/kɛtʃt/ (pret. of *catch*) 10
kind of (intensive) 72-73
kneel (inf.) 21
kneeled (pret.) 21, 85 (ppl.) 21
knelt (pret.) 21 (ppl.) 21
know (inf.) 79
knowed (pret.) 79 (ppl.) 79
Kurath, Hans 64

laid (pret.) 21-22
lay (pret.) 21-22
lay (intr.) 85
learn (inf.) 21, 30 (pret.) 21
learned (pret.) 21, 85. F11, 21
learnt (pret.) 21, 83. F11, 21
lie (inf.) 21-22 (pret.) 22
lied (pret.) 22
like (conj.) 61-62
'll = will 45-46
look here! 76-77
look-a-here! 76-77. F50, 76
look-it-here! 76-77, 83. F50, 76
looky-here! 76-77. F50, 76
lynk = lynx 80

Marckwardt, Albert H. 50, 71
McDavid, Raven I., Jr. 4, 50
McDavid, Virginia Glenn 4, 14, 31, 50, 84
me (1st sg. post-*be*) 56-57, 85
middlin' (intensive) 73. F46, 73
might (pret.) 22
might be able 46
might could = might be able 46
more (adj.) —er 81
moth (pl.) 48. F29, 48
/mɔθ/ = moths 48. F29, 48
/mɔθs/ = moths 48. F29, 48

name after (him) 63
name for (him) 63. F36, 63
neither am/will/would I 78
never (—) no 81
never ought to 42. F26, 42
never used to (neg. 3d sg. pret.) 39-40
nor am/will I 78
nor I 78
nor I either 77-78
nor I (n)either 78
nor me (n)either 78
not (—) never 81
not (—) no 81

of (the stomach) 65
(quarter) of 67
off (prep.) 67-68
(want) off 71-72
off from = off 68. F41, 68
off of 68. F41, 68
off'm = off 68. F41, 68
off'n = off 67-68, 85-86. F41, 68
on account of = because 61. F34, 61
on/onto 68
on purpose 71
ought not (neg. 3d sg.) 41-42
oughtn't (neg. sg.) 42-43, 85

ours (1st pl. geni-
   tive) 54
(want) out 72. F45,
   72
over nigh 75
over yonder 74-75.
   F49, 75
*Oxford English Dic-
   tionary* 26, 31,
   71, 81

pair(s) (pl.) 52
past (prep.) 68-69
poison (adj.) 58.
   F32, 58
poisonous 58. F32, 58
pound(s) (pl.) 51,
   85. F30, 51
pretty (intensive)
   73. F46, 73
purposely 71

quarter from/to/till
   67
Quirk, Randolph 82
quite (intensive) 73

raised (pret. of
   rise) 23, 84-86.
   F12, 23
ran (pret.) 24
rather (intensive)
   72-73. F46, 73
reach (pret.) 79
rech (pret. of *reach*)
   79
remember of 80
rid (ppl. of *ride*)
   23, 86
ridden (ppl.) 22-23
ride (inf.) 22
rise (inf.) 23
rised (pret.) 23, 84,
   86. F12, 23
rode (ppl.) 23, 84-85
rose (pret.) 23
ruin (inf.) 35
ruint (pret.) 79
run (inf.) 24
   (pret.) 24, 85

-s (3d sg. pres.) 34,
   79-80
sang (ppl.) 79
sat (pret.) 26-27
saw (pret.) 25
scairt (pret.) 24-25,

85. F13, 25
seed (pret.) 25, 83,
   86. F14, 25; F52,
   83
seen (pret.) 25, 84-
   85
set (imp.) 26-27
   (pret.) 27, 83, 85.
   F16, 27
shafts (pl.) 48-49
/ʃæfs/ = shafts 48-49
/ʃæfts/ = shafts 48-
   49
/ʃævz/ = shafts 48-49
shake it up! 74
shall (1st sg.) 45-46
   (1st pl.) 46
sheeps (pl.) 80
shouldn't (neg. sg.)
   42
shrank (pret.) 26.
   F15, 26
shrink (inf.) 26
shrinked 86
shrunk (pret.) 26
sick at the/one's
   stomach 60
sick in the stomach
   86
sick on the stomach
   86
sick to (etc.) the
   stomach 64-65
sing (inf.) 79
sit (inf. or imp.)
   26-27
   (pret.) 27. F16, 27
sleep (inf.) 79
slep (pret.) 79
sort of (intensive)
   72-73. F46, 73
sot (pret.) 27, 84,
   86. F16, 27
span(s) (pl.) 52
spoil (inf.) 27
spoiled (ppl. adj.)
   27-28
spoilt (ppl. adj.)
   27-28, 83, 85. F17,
   28
srunk = shrunk 83
start (inf.) 8
started (pret.) 8
*Studies in Languages
   and Linguistics in
   Honor of Charles C.
   Fries* 50
swam (pret.) 28-29
swear (inf.) 79
sweat (inf.) 28
   (pret.) 28. F18, 28
sweated 85
swim (inf.) 28
swimmed (pret.) 85

swore (ppl.) 79
swum (pret.) 29, 83-
   85. F19, 29

take (inf.) 29
taken (pret.) 29, 83,
   86. F52, 83
   (ppl.) 29
taught (pret.) 29-30
teach (inf.) 29
team(s) (pl.) 52
tear (inf.) 30
tell (inf.) 45
that (conj.) 61-62
that (rel. pron.) 55-
   56, 85
that he = that 55-56
that his = whose 56,
   85
the/∅ 60
the/one's 60
theirn 54-55. F31, 54
theirs (3d pl.) 54
theirselves 81
them = those 58-59,
   81, 85
themself 81
they = there 80
this way 73-74
this-a-way 73-74, 86.
   F47, 74
those (dem. adj.) 58-
   59
those kind of 80-81
though (conj.) 61-62
threw (pret.) 30
throw (inf.) 30
throwed (pret.) 30-
   31. F20, 30
   (ppl.) 31
(quarter) till 67.
   F40, 67
time's a-wastin'! 74
to (the stomach) 64-
   65. F38, 65
(quarter) to 67
to home 64, 86. F37,
   64
took (pret.) 29
   (ppl.) 29, 86
tore (ppl.) 30, 85
torn (ppl.) 30
toward(s) (prep.)
   69
troth = trough (sg.)
   49
troughs (pl.) 49
/trɔfs/· = troughs 49
/trɔθ/ = troughs 49
/trɔθs/ = troughs 49
/trɔðz/ = troughs 49
/trɔvz/ = troughs 49

tuck (pret. of *take*)
   29, 86

unless (conj.) 62
up yonder 75
us (nom.) 80
used not to (neg. 3d
   sg. pret.) 39-40
used to could 80
usen't to (neg. 3d
   sg. pret.) 39-40,
   85

wait for/on 66
wait on 83. F52, 83
wake (inf.) 31
   (pret.) 31
waked (pret.) 31
wakened 31, 85
want in 72. F45, 72
want off 71-72, 83.
   F44, 72
want out 72. F45, 72
want to get off 71-72
wants to come in 72.
   F45, 72
warn't (neg. 3d sg.
   pret. of *be*) 43, 85
was (pl.) 34-35, 85
wash (the) dishes 60.
   F33, 60
wasn't (neg. 3d sg.
   pret.) 43
way yonder 75
way(s) (pl.) 50
we (obj.) 80
wear (inf.) 31
went (ppl.) 79
were (pl.) 34-35
what = that 55-56
what (interrog. pl.
   or collective) 54
what-all (interrog.
   pl. or collective)
   54
what-all's (3d pl.
   genitive) 55
whether (omitted) 81-
   82
who (interrog. pl.)
   53
who (rel. pron.) 55-
   56, 85
who-all (interrog.
   pl.) 53-54
who-all's (2d pl.
   genitive) 55
whose (rel. pron.
   genitive) 56, 85
will (1st sg.) 45-46
   (1st pl.) 46

will not (neg. 1st
  sg. pres.) 43
with (the stomach) 65
without = unless 62,
  85, 86. F35, 62
woke (pret.) 31, 85
won't (neg. 1st sg.
  pres.) 43
/wɑnt/ = won't 43

/wɚnt/ = wasn't 43
/wɔnt/ = won't 43.
  F27, 43
/wont/ = won't 43.
  F27, 43
/wunt/ = won't 43.
  F27, 43
/wʌnt/ = won't 43.
  F27, 43

wore (ppl.) 31-32,
  85
worn (ppl.) 31-32
writ (pret.) 32
write (inf.) 32
written (ppl.)
  32
wrote (ppl.) 32,
  84-85. F21, 32

yoke(s) (pl.) 51-
  52
yonder 75, 85-86.
  F49, 75
you (2d pl.) 53
you-all 53, 83, 85.
  F52, 83
youse (2d pl.) 53,
  83, 85